كتاب التوحيد الذي هو حق الله علي العبيد

THE BOOK OF TAWHID

THE RIGHT OF ALLĀH UPON HIS SERVANT

VOLUME I

CHAPTER 1 — CHAPTER 29

by the Imām Muhammad b. 'Abdul-Wahhab b. Sulaymān b. 'Ali al-Tamimī al-Najdi

WORKBOOK EDITION

DETAILED VERIFICATION OF NARRATIONS

INCLUDES 145 QUESTIONS AND ANSWERS

ARABIC TEXT TAKEN FROM VERIFIED MANUSCRIPTS

PUBLISHED BY:
DAAR AL-WAALID (LONDON, UK) *alongside* AL-ATHARIYYAH (LONDON, UK)

EMAIL:
daaralwaalid@gmail.com

ADDRESS:
Masjid Abdul-Aziz Bin Bāz, East Road, London, E15 3QR

TWITTER:
@uwaysT
@Athariyyah

Translated and Compiled by Abu Abdur-Rahman Uways at-Taweel, Kevin Onwordi

Table of Contents

Preface: Translator's Introduction 7

- START OF MAIN TEXT -

Introduction: The Book of At-Tawhīd 19

Chapter 1: The Virtues of at-Tawhīd and Its Expiation of Sins 31

Chapter 2: Whoever Establishes at-Tawhīd Enters Paradise without Being Taken to Account 41

Chapter 3: The Fear of Falling into Shirk 51

Chapter 4: The Call to the Testification that None Deserves to be Worshiped in Except Allāh 59

Chapter 5: The Explanation of Tawhid and The Testimony of Lā ilāhā illā Allāh 69

Chapter 6: Wearing a Ring, Twine, and its Likes for Prevention or Lifting of Harm is an Act of Shirk 79

Chapter 7: What Has Come Regarding Ruqā, Talismans and Amulets 87

Chapter 8: Whoever Seeks Blessings Through a Tree, a Stone, or the Like 99

Chapter 9: Slaughtering for Other than Allāh 107

Chapter 10: No Sacrifice for Allah Should be Done in a Place Where Sacrifice for Others is Made 119

Chapter 11: To Vow to Other Than Allāh is an Act of Shirk 125

Chapter 12: From Shirk is to Seek Refuge in Other Than Allah 131

Chapter 13: From Shirk is to Seek Deliverance from Other than Allah or Invoke Other than Him 137

Chapter 14: "Do they ascribe partners with Allāh — those who created nothing but they themselves are created? No help can they give them..." 147

Chapter 15: "Until such time as fear is banished from their hearts..." 157

Chapter 16: Intercession 167

Chapter 17: "Verily, you do not guide whom you like..." 179

Chapter 18: Exaggeration in the Righteous is the Root Cause for Mankind's Disbelief and Leaving the Religion 187

Chapter 19: Condemnation of the One Who Worships Allah at a Righteous Man's Grave. What if he actually Worships the Man! 197

Chapter 20: Exaggeration of Righteous People's Graves Leads to them Being idols Worshipped besides Allāh 207

Chapter 21: The Protectiveness of Al-Mustafa ( ) of Tawhid and his Blocking of Paths Leading to Shirk 215

Chapter 22: Some People of this Ummah (Nation) will worship Idols 221

Chapter 23: The Chapter on Sorcery and Magic 233

Chapter 24: Clarification on Some Types of Magic 243

Chapter 25: What Has Come Regarding Soothsayers and the Like 253

PREFACE:

Translator's Introduction

بسم الله الرحمن الرحيم

Verily, all praise is for Allāh, we praise Him, seek His assistance and we ask for His forgiveness. And we seek refuge in Allāh from the evils of ourselves and the evils of our actions.

Whomsoever Allah guides, none can lead him astray, and whoever has been led astray, there is no guide for him. I bear witness that no deity has the right to be worshipped except Allāh — alone and with no partners- and I bear witness that Muḥammad is His slave and Messenger (صَلَّى ٱللَّهُ عَلَيْهِ وَسَلَّمَ).

> "O you who believe, fear Allāh as He ought to be feared and do not die except as Muslims." [Sūrah Al Imrān: 102]
>
> ••
>
> "O mankind, fear Allāh who created you from a single soul (Ādam) and created from that, its mate (Eve). And from both of them, He brought forth many men and women. And fear Allāh to whom you demand your mutual rights. Verily, Allāh is an All-Watcher over you." [Sūrah An-Nisā: 1]
>
> ••
>
> "O you who believe, fear Allāh and speak a precise word (i.e. truthful). He will rectify your deeds for you and forgive you your sins. And whoever obeys Allāh and His Messenger has indeed achieved a great success." [Surah Al-Ahzab: 70-71]

To proceed: The best speech is the Speech of Allāh. The best example and guidance is that of the Messenger (صَلَّى ٱللَّهُ عَلَيْهِ وَسَلَّمَ). The evillest affairs are the newly invented matters in the religion. Every newly invented matter in the religion is bid'ah (heresy), which is in of itself deviance and every deviance leads to the Hellfire.

That which follows is a compiled workbook of the famous, monumental book *The Book of Tawḥīd: The Rights of Allāh Upon His Servant*. Authored by the Imām Muḥammad b. 'Abdil-Wahhāb (رَحِمَهُ ٱللَّهُ).

The text has been formatted into a workbook that can be used by a student of knowledge for note-taking whilst listening to explanations of the original text. Useful for conferences and courses where the book is being taught. The footnotes and end-of-chapter questions add an extra element to the book where educators and students alike can study the verses and prophetic traditions in its detailed form.

Who is the author of the original book?

He is the Imām Muḥammad b. 'Abdul-Wahhāb b. Sulaymān b. 'Alī b. At-Tamimī An-Najdī. He was born in a village called Al-'Uyaynah in the year 1115H (1701M). After a long life in seeking knowledge, teaching, and calling to Islām and the Sunnah, he died in the year 1207H at the age of 92. May Allāh have mercy and reward him with paradise for his efforts.

What is the name of the original text of the book?

Various names have been given to this book;

1. (كتاب التوحيد): *'The Book of Tawḥīd'* (Islamic Monotheism). This name was given because the author (رَحِمَهُ ٱللَّهُ) mentioned this in the introductory section of his book, albeit not specifically as a title where he said: *'The Book of Tawḥīd and the statement of Allāh'*. This name was also mentioned by his offspring who authored renowned explanations of the text. They mentioned the name in the preludes. Namely *Taysīr al-Azīz al-Ḥamīd* by the scholar of ḥadīth Sh. Sulaymān b. 'Abdillāh b. Muḥammad b. 'Abdil-Wahhāb; the grandson of the author. Also, *Fat-ḥul-Majīd*.

2. (كتاب التوحيد الذي هو حق الله على العبيد): *'The Book of Tawḥīd - The Rights of Allāh Upon His Servant'*. This is the name that is the most widespread amongst scholars. This specific title has variations with differing prepositions. However, they all revolve around this meaning. This was the title mentioned specifically by the students of the author and his children. The earliest manuscripts also have this as the name of the book. Therefore, this name is the most widespread and chosen name for this exemplary work. Therefore, all the other names ascribed to this book fall under this title: *The Book of Tawḥīd - The Rights of Allāh Upon His Servant.*

Where and when was this book authored?

Scholars differed as to where the book was authored. Sh. 'Abdur-Raḥmān Āalī as-Shaykh mentions that it was authored in the city of al-Baṣrah, in 'Irāq. This was when the author sought knowledge there. He witnessed many acts of shirk, innovation, and deviance which led him to author this book. Others have stated that he wrote the book in Ḥuraimalāa when he returned from 'Irāq. This has been mentioned by ibn Ghannām and Sh. 'Abdul-Laṭīf b. 'Abdi-Raḥmān Āalīas-Shaykh.

In combining these two opinions it can be said that the book was authored in al-Baṣrah, 'Irāq then the point-form summary (issues) at the end of each chapter was written on his return to an-Najd who were more advanced in the knowledge of the religion.

In addition, the majority of the residents of al-Baṣrah were ignorant and fanatical as it relates to the family of the Prophet (صَلَّى ٱللَّهُ عَلَيْهِ وَسَلَّمَ). This could be the reason why the author mentions the majority of narrations narrated from the family of the Messenger (صَلَّى ٱللَّهُ عَلَيْهِ وَسَلَّمَ). For example, from the narrations he placed in this book five (5) were from 'Alī b. Abī Ṭālib (رَضِيَ ٱللَّهُ عَنْهُ) and twenty-four (24) were from 'Abdullāh b. 'Abbās (رَضِيَ ٱللَّهُ عَنْهُمَا), one (1) from 'Abbās b. 'Abdul-Muṭṭalib (رَضِيَ ٱللَّهُ عَنْهُ) and one (1) from 'Alī b. al-Ḥusayn (رَحِمَهُ ٱللَّهُ). Also, that which is notable is that when he quotes from Shaykh al-Islām ibn Taymiyyah, he usually calls him Abū al-'Abbās as the name 'Abbās was more beloved to them as it is a name of some of the family members of the Messenger (صَلَّى ٱللَّهُ عَلَيْهِ وَسَلَّمَ).

As for when the book was authored, then if we hold that he wrote the book during his travels to al-Baṣrah, it would have been between the year (1137H) and (1139H). This was the period he resided in al-Baṣrah at the age of 24. However, if we hold that he wrote the book in Ḥuraimalā, it has been documented that he publicly propagated the call to tawḥīd after the death of his father in the year (1153H) at the age of 37. In any case, that which is established is that he wrote this book in the early years of his adult life (رَحِمَهُ ٱللَّهُ).[1]

Can we have a synopsis of this book?

Al- Imām Muḥammad b. 'Abdul-Wahhāb authored this book predominantly based on the Tawḥīd of Worship. He covers the essence of worshiping Allāh alone without any partners and warning against its opposite which is shirk (polytheism).

The introduction of the book deals with the importance of at-Tawḥīd; that Allāh created the jinn and humankind to worship Him alone without any partners. The author brings verses from the Qur'ān to show that all the Messengers (عَلَيْهِمُ ٱلسَّلَامُ) called to at-Tawḥīd and were all sent with that message. After that, he mentions the obligation of disbelieving in false deities. Then, he mentions the narration of Mu'ādh b. Jabal (رَضِيَ ٱللَّهُ عَنْهُ). This is the consistent methodology of the shaykh (رَحِمَهُ ٱللَّهُ) throughout this exemplary book. He references each chapter with verses from the Qur'ān and (or) narrations from the Sunnah.

He then mentions the virtues of implementing at-Tawḥīd; as the one who realizes the virtues of something will race to it. In the chapters that follow, he goes into detail

1 — 'Unwān al-Majd: 1/30

Buḥūth Nadwa D'awatu as-Shaykh: 1/79. See Kitāb at-Tawḥīd- Maktabah Ahl-Athar; Fifth Edition: 20-22 regarding the affair of at-Tawḥīd. Herein, closing this portion of the book with the virtues of calling and propagating at-Tawḥīd.[1]

The following chapters highlight the dangers and harms of polytheism (shirk) in its various forms. By this, the one with intellect will distance themselves from falling into shirk and ask Allāh for protection and guidance. The shaykh then mentions how the Messenger (صَلَّى ٱللَّهُ عَلَيْهِ وَسَلَّمَ) protected the side of at-Tawḥīd through various narrations. Thereafter, the author mentions various chapters about caution and protectiveness over the affair of at-Tawḥīd.

The author then mentions a few chapters about the names and attributes of Allāh. These chapters show proof that the belief in the names and attributes necessitates that Allāh alone deserves to be worshipped without equals nor partners. Even though this book is generally on the Tawḥīd of worship, all three categories of tawḥīd are covered in certain chapters making this book the first of its kind as it relates to the organization of its chapters and emphasis on the tawḥīd of worship. The book is then befittingly sealed with The Chapter regarding Allah's Statement: "*They did not make a just estimate of Allāh in that which He deserves. On the Day of Resurrection, the whole of the earth will be grasped by His Hand.*" [39:67]

Al-Imām Ibn al-Qayyim said: "No one receives the threat of punishment and actual punishment as much as the people of shirk. They have bad thoughts of Allāh which led them to associate partners with Him. If they had good thoughts of Allāh, they would have singled Him out alone in worship. This is why Allāh mentioned regarding the polytheists that they did not make a just estimate of Him that which He deserves in three places in the Qur'ān." [6:91,39:67, 22: 74][1]

Books that were authored afterwards on the subject have been greatly influenced by this scholastic work.[2]

What have scholars said regarding this book?

Shaykh Sulaymān b. 'Abdullāh (1233h) (رَحِمَهُ ٱللَّهُ) said: "It is a unique book on its subject. No book has been authored like it before and books after it cannot be compared to it."[3]

Shaykh 'Abdur-Raḥmān b. Ḥasan (1275h) (رَحِمَهُ ٱللَّهُ) said: "Even in its concise nature, he(the author) compiled within it much good. It incorporates pieces of evidence on

1 — Ighāthatul-Lahfān: 1/61

2 — Ḥāshiyah Kitāb at-Tawhīd by 'Abdur-Raḥmān b. Qāsim: (406)

3 — Taysīr al-'Azīz al-Ḥamīd: (24)

at-Tawhid that which is sufficient for the one whom Allāh guides. He has mentioned proofs on the clarification of as-Shirk, the sin Allāh does not forgive."[1]

The historian, Shaykh 'Uthman b.'Abdillah b. Bishr (1290h) (رَحِمَهُ ٱللَّهُ) said: "No author has written on the subject of at-Tawhīd better than this book. Indeed, the author excelled in this authorship and gave justice to the topic." [2]

Shaykh Sulayman b. Ḥamdān (1397h) (رَحِمَهُ ٱللَّهُ) said: "In every chapter (of this book) is a principle from the principles in which much benefit is found. The majority of those in his (the author's) generation fell into major and minor shirk. They deemed their actions as being from the religion so neither did they repent from it nor seek forgiveness from Allah. Therefore, the author wrote this book based on that which he witnessed, so the book became a cure for those illnesses (i.e. minor and major shirk)." [3]

Shaykh 'Abdullāh al-Jār Allāh (1414h) (رَحِمَهُ ٱللَّهُ) said: "He Muḥammad b. 'Abdul-Wahhāb) has authored many valuable books and from the most important of them is this priceless book which is from the most important written on the topic of at-Tawḥīd."[4]

The Grand Muftī Shaykh 'Abdul-'Azīz b. Bāz (1420h) (رَحِمَهُ ٱللَّهُ) said: "I advise my brothers, the students of knowledge to focus along with the Qur'ān and Sunnah, books of creed. They should memorize that which they can from these books. They are the foundations (of all sciences) and a summary of that which is in the Qur'ān and Sunnah. An example of these books is *The Book of at-Tawḥīd* which was authored by Shaykh-ul-Islām Muḥammād 'Abul-Wahhāb, May Allāh have mercy on him."[5]

The revivor of the Sunnah in Yemen Shaykh Muqbil b. Hādī (1422h) (رَحِمَهُ ٱللَّهُ) said: "From the most valuable books that no Muslim can do without is... *The Book of at-Tawhid* by Shaykh Muhammad b. 'Abdul-Wahhāb, May Allāh have mercy upon him."[6]

Shaykh Ṣāliḥ al-Fawzān said: "This book is from the most precious authored on the topic of at-Tawhid. This is because in of itself it is based on the Book (Qur'ān) and Sunnah."[7]

1 — Ad-Durr as-Sinniyyah: 3/169

2 — 'Unwān al-Majd: 1/185

3 — Ad-Dur an-Naḍīd: (5)

4 — Al-Jām'I al-Farīd: (6)

5 — 'Iyanah al-'Ulamah fi Kitāb at-Tawḥīd: 42

6 — Al-Mukhtarah: 138

7 — I'ānah al-Mustafīd: 1/18

How many chapters are there in this book?

In some prints of this book, there are 67 chapters. However, the first chapter is widely considered as an introduction to the book. Therefore, in this workbook, we have an introduction and 66 chapters. The text has been verified and compared and contrasted with various manuscript copies from the author and early explanations of this pioneering book.

How many verses from the Qur'ān are used as evidence in this book?

This Imām mentions 80 Qur'ānic verses in this book as evidence for most of his chapters.

How many narrations are referred to in this book?

This book is full of narrations from the Messenger (ﷺ). There are 141 narrations used as primary and secondary evidence for the majority of the chapters; 34 agreed upon by al-Bukhārī and Muslim with repetition, 17 reported by al-Bukhārī alone, 23 by Muslim, and 74 other narrations from Abī Dāwūd, At-Tirmidhī, An-Nasā'ī, the Musnad of al-Imām Aḥmad Ibn Mājah and others. As for statements of the companions and other than them from the early generations and after, there are 57 quotes. Therefore, this book has been authored with close referencing to the Qur'ān and Sunnah based on the understanding of the pious early generations.

How do we understand the mentioning of weak narrations found in this book?

As one studies this fundamental book, they will find several narrations are weak due to its chain of narrators. Whilst the discrepancies of the narrations are mentioned in the footnotes of this workbook, it is to be noted that the weak narrations that are mentioned can be either linked to a Quranic verse or another authentic narration in that particular chapter with similar and at times identical meanings.[1]

Shaykh Al-Islām Ibn Taymiyyah (رَحِمَهُ ٱللَّهُ) said regarding occasions when scholars have references to weak narrations in their works: "It is not used as a fundamental proof but mentioned along with other fundamental texts that are authentic and free from discrepancies to show that the meaning of that weak narration is correct."

1 — *Ar-Radd 'alā al-Bakrī*: 118

Al-Allāmah Al-Fawzān said: " There is not a mention of a narration in this book except that it is either authentic, acceptable, strengthened by other narrations or supporting fundamental texts from the Qur'ān and Sunnah." [1]

Knowledge of this is imperative in grasping the comprehensive benefits of this book.

Study Guidelines

1. The Quranic verses are strictly referenced.

2. The narrations found in al-Bukhārī and Muslim are referenced. If there are narrations from other than al-Bukhārī and Muslim, they have been graded with reference to the scholars of ḥadīth from either the past and present or both.

3. The sources for referenced books are all from Arabic literature.

4. The conclusion of each chapter has 5 questions related to its chapter. This is based on the main and sub-objectives of the chapter, benefits, and Issues (points) mentioned in the original text. The intent behind this to make this a good resource for both teacher and student.

5. Writing space has been distributed according to the benefits and branching issues that can be extrapolated from each sectioned part of the text.

After this, I ask Allāh the Most High to reward Al-Imām Muḥammad 'Abdul-Wahhāb (رَحِمَهُ ٱللَّهُ) with the utmost good for this monumental book on Islamic Monotheism. May Allāh bless this workbook and make it be for His sake making it of benefit for mankind and a means of forgiveness for its needy compiler.

Abū 'Abdir-Raḥmān Uways Onwordi (at-Taweel)

28-02-1442 H — 28-10-2020 CE

1 — See *al-'I'ānah al-Mustafīd* :1/12

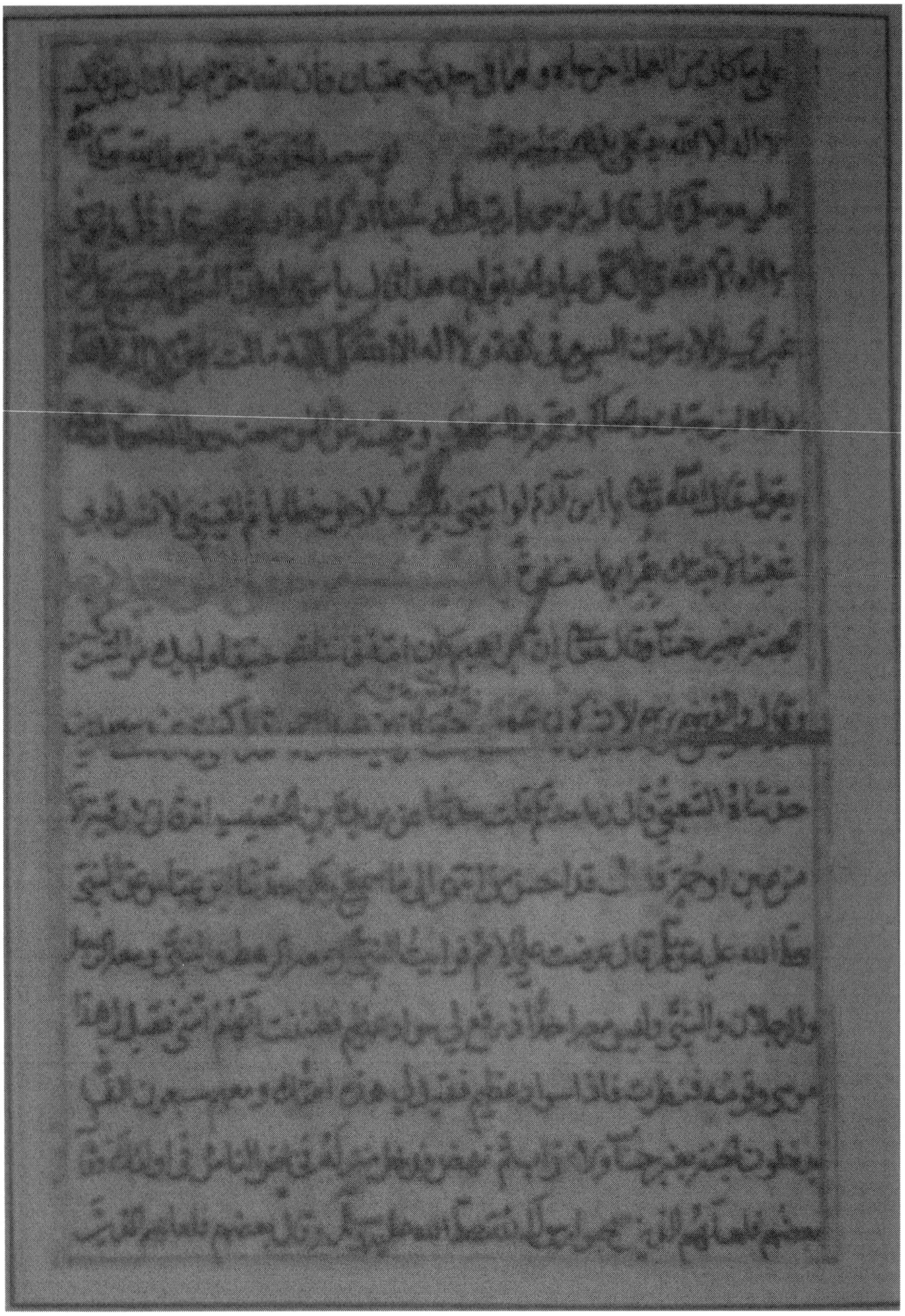

The first page from the foundational relied upon manuscript of Kitāb at-Tawhid handwritien by the author's grandson as-Shaykh Sulaimān.

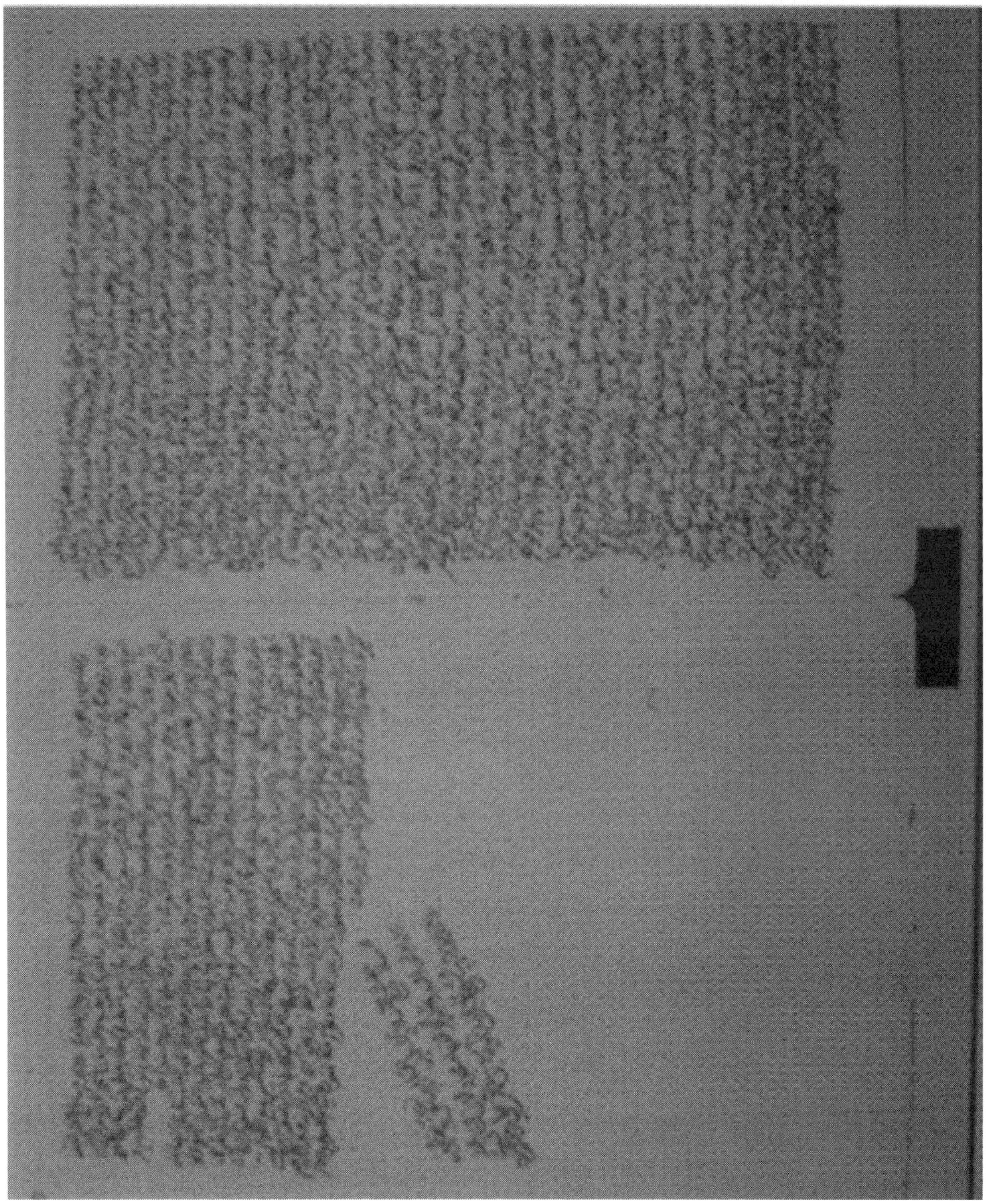

Claimed handwriting of al-Imām Muḥammad b 'Abdul-Wahhāb taken from his book collection.

A title cover handwritten by the grandson of the author; Shaykh Sulaiman b.'Abdullāh b. Muḥammad 'Abdul-Wahhāb.[1]

1 — See Kitāb at-Tawḥīd- Maktabah Ahl-Athar; Fifth Edition.

كتاب التوحيد الذي هو حق الله على العبيد

The Book of Tawhīd Clarifying 'The Rights of Allāh Upon His Servant'

By al-Imām Muhammad b. 'Abdil-Wahhāb

- START OF MAIN TEXT -

A workbook compiled and referenced
by Abū Abdur-Raḥmān Uways At-Taweel

INTRODUCTION:

The Book of At-Tawhīd

وَقَوْلِ اللهِ تَعَالَى: ﴿وَمَا خَلَقْتُ الْجِنَّ وَالْإِنسَ إِلَّا لِيَعْبُدُونِ﴾ الذاريات: ٥٦

Allāh said: "And I (Allāh) did not create the Jinn and humankind except they should worship Me (Alone)." (51:56)

وَقَوْلِه: ﴿وَلَقَدْ بَعَثْنَا فِي كُلِّ أُمَّةٍ رَّسُولًا أَنِ اعْبُدُوا اللَّهَ وَاجْتَنِبُوا الطَّاغُوتَ﴾ النحل: ٣٦

He also said: "And verily, We have sent to every nation a Messenger (proclaiming): 'Worship Allāh (Alone), and stay away from all false deities.'" [16:36]

وَقَوْلِه: ﴿وَقَضَىٰ رَبُّكَ أَلَّا تَعْبُدُوا إِلَّا إِيَّاهُ وَبِالْوَالِدَيْنِ إِحْسَانًا﴾ الإسراء: ٢٣

He said: "And your Lord has decreed that you worship none but Him. And that you be dutiful to your parents." [17:23]

وَقَوْلِه: ﴿وَاعْبُدُوا اللَّهَ وَلَا تُشْرِكُوا بِهِ شَيْئًا﴾ النساء: ٣٦

He said: "Worship Allāh and do not associate anything with Him in worship." (4:36)

وَقَوْلِه: ﴿قُلْ تَعَالَوْا أَتْلُ مَا حَرَّمَ رَبُّكُمْ عَلَيْكُمْ ۖ أَلَّا تُشْرِكُوا بِهِ شَيْئًا ۖ وَبِالْوَالِدَيْنِ إِحْسَانًا﴾ الأنعام: ١٥١

He also said: "Say (O Muhammad ﷺ): Come, I will recite to you what your Lord has prohibited for you: Do not join anything in worship with Him; be good and dutiful to your parents..." [6: 151-153]

قَالَ ابْنُ مَسْعُودٍ رَضِيَٱللَّهُعَنْهُ: مَنْ أَرَادَ أَنْ يَنْظُرَ إِلَى وَصِيَّةِ مُحَمَّدٍ صَلَّىٱللَّهُعَلَيْهِوَسَلَّمَ الَّتِي عَلَيْهَا خَاتَمُهُ فَلْيَقْرَأْ قَوْلَهُ تَعَالَى « قُلْ تَعَالَوْا أَتْلُ مَا حَرَّمَ رَبُّكُمْ عَلَيْكُمْ أَلَّا تُشْرِكُوا بِهِ شَيْئًا » إِلَى قَوْلِهِ: « وَأَنَّ هَٰذَا صِرَاطِي مُسْتَقِيمًا » الأنعام: ١٥١–١٥٣

Ibn Mas`ūd (رَضِيَٱللَّهُعَنْهُ) said: “Whoever wishes to ascertain the very bequeath of Prophet Muhammad (صَلَّىٱللَّهُعَلَيْهِوَسَلَّمَ) on which the Prophet (صَلَّىٱللَّهُعَلَيْهِوَسَلَّمَ) has put His seal on, let him read the Statement of Allāh: *‘Say (O Muhammad صَلَّىٱللَّهُعَلَيْهِوَسَلَّمَ): Come, I will recite what your Lord has prohibited for you: Do join not anything in worship with Him...’* — up to: *‘...And verily, this is My Straight Path...’”* [Al-An`ām : 151-153] [1]

1 — At-Tirmidhī: (3070) This narration has been deemed weak due to the narrator Dāwūd al-Awdī. Scholars differed regarding who he is . The correct opinion is that he is Abu Yazīd who is weak. Deemed weak by al-Imām Ahmad, Abū Dāwūd and others. (Mīzānal-I`tidāl: 1/375).

وَعَنْ مُعَاذِ بْنِ جَبَلٍ رَضِيَ اللَّهُ عَنْهُ قَالَ: كُنْتُ رَدِيفَ النَّبِيِّ صَلَّى اللَّهُ عَلَيْهِ وَسَلَّمَ عَلَى حِمَارٍ، فَقَالَ لِي: «يَا مُعَاذُ أَتَدْرِي مَا حَقُّ اللهِ عَلَى الْعِبَادِ؟، وَمَا حَقُّ الْعِبَادِ عَلَى اللهِ؟»، قُلْتُ: اللهُ وَرَسُولُهُ أَعْلَمُ، قَالَ: «حَقُّ اللهِ عَلَى الْعِبَادِ: أَنْ يَعْبُدُوهُ وَلَا يُشْرِكُوا بِهِ شَيْئًا، وَحَقُّ الْعِبَادِ عَلَى اللهِ: أَنْ لَا يُعَذِّبَ مَنْ لَا يُشْرِكُ بِهِ شَيْئًا»، قُلْتُ: يَا رَسُولَ اللهِ؛ أَفَلَا أُبَشِّرُ النَّاسَ؟ قَالَ: «لَا تُبَشِّرْهُمْ فَيَتَّكِلُوا». أَخْرَجَاهُ فِي الصَّحِيحَيْنِ.

It is narrated that Mu`ādh bin Jabal (رَضِيَ اللَّهُ عَنْهُ) said: I was riding behind the Prophet (صَلَّى اللَّهُ عَلَيْهِ وَسَلَّمَ) on a donkey and he said to me: "O Mu`ādh, do you know what is the right of Allāh upon his slaves and the right of the slaves upon Allāh?" I responded: "Allāh and His Messenger know best." He continued, "The Right of Allāh upon His slaves is to worship Him Alone and to never associate anything with him. The right of slaves upon Him is to not punish any person who does not associate anything with Him." I said: "O Allāh's Messenger (صَلَّى اللَّهُ عَلَيْهِ وَسَلَّمَ), shall I give glad tidings to the people?" He replied: "No! Do not inform them, lest they rely on it (and become complacent)." (Al-Bukhārī and Muslim) [1]

1 — Al-Bukhārī: (2856, 5967, 6267, 6500, 7373) , Muslim: (30) and Ahmad: (36/318)

ISSUES OF THIS CHAPTER:

1. The wisdom of Allāh in creating jinn and mankind.

2. Worship is Tawḥīd, as, in this issue, there had always been dispute (between the Prophets and the polytheists).

3. Those who have not fulfilled the requirements of Tawḥīd are such as they have not worshipped Allāh, and in this sense is the meaning of the verse:

> "Nor will you worship that which I worship." (109:3).

4. The wisdom in sending the Messengers.

5. The message of the Prophet (ﷺ) (Tawḥīd) applies to all nations.

6. All Prophets have brought the same religion.

7. The major issue is that the worship of Allāh cannot be performed until Ṭāghūt is denounced and rejected. This is the meaning of the saying of Allāh:

> "Whoever disbelieves in Ṭāghūt and believes in Allāh then he has grasped the most trustworthy handhold."(2:256)

8. At-Ṭāghūt is inclusive of all that is worshipped other than Allāh.

9. The tremendous importance of the three entirely clear verses of Surah Al-An'am (6:151-153) among the early pious predecessors. In these verses are 10 issues, the first of which is the prohibition of Shirk.

10. The clear verses in Surah Al-Isra (17:22-39) have 18 substantial issues. Allāh begins them with:

> "Do not set up with Allāh any other diety, (O man) or you will sit down reproved, forsaken (in the Hell-fire)".(17:22)

And ended with:

> "And do not set up with Allāh any other diety lest you should be thrown into Hell, blameworthy and rejected." (17:39).
>
> "This is (part) of Al-Hikmah (wisdom, good manners, and high character, etc.) which your Lord has inspired to you." (17:39)

ISSUES OF THIS CHAPTER:

The verse of Surah An-Nisaa (4:36) called "The verse of the ten rights" to which Allāh the Most High begins by saying:

> "And worship Allāh, and join none with Him in worship."

We must note the admonition of Prophet Muḥammad (صَلَّى ٱللَّٰهُ عَلَيْهِ وَسَلَّمَ) which he made before his death.

11. To recognize Allāh's right upon us.

12. To recognize the rights of slaves on Allāh, if they fulfill His right.

13. This issue was unknown to most of the Companions of Prophet Muḥammad (صَلَّى ٱللَّٰهُ عَلَيْهِ وَسَلَّمَ).

14. Permissibility to hide some knowledge for the legislative good.

15. It is desirable to pass the pleasing news to other Muslims.

16. Fear of depending (and being complacent) upon the expansiveness of Allāh's mercy.

17. The statement of one, who is asked on matters that are not known to him: "Allāh and His Messenger know best."

18. It is correct to impart knowledge selectively to some and not to others.

19. The humility of Prophet Muḥammad (صَلَّى ٱللَّٰهُ عَلَيْهِ وَسَلَّمَ) on riding a donkey with a companion behind.

20. It is permissible to have a second rider behind.

21. The seriousness of this affair.

22. The virtue of Mu`ādh (رَضِيَ ٱللَّٰهُ عَنْهُ).

CHAPTER EXERCISES

1. What is the wisdom behind the creation of the jinn and humankind? What is the evidence for your answer?

2. What is the wisdom behind Allāh sending the Messengers? Give one evidence for your answer.

3. What is the difference between the rights of Allāh upon his servants and the rights of the servants upon Allāh?

4. Why did Allāh mention dutifulness to the parents after at-At-Tawhīd in the same verse?

5. Which narration in this chapter gives us an example of the humility of the Messenger of Allāh (صَلَّى ٱللَّهُ عَلَيْهِ وَسَلَّمَ)?

CHAPTER EXERCISES

CHAPTER EXERCISES

CHAPTER 1:

The Virtues of at-Tawhīd and Its Expiation of Sins

وَقَـوْلِ اللـهِ تَعَالَـى: «الَّذِيـنَ آمَنُـوا وَلَـمْ يَلْبِسُـوا إِيمَانَهُـم بِظُلْـمٍ أُولَٰئِـكَ لَهُـمُ الْأَمْـنُ وَهُـم مُّهْتَـدُونَ»
الأنعام: ٨٢

He said: "Those who believe (in the Oneness of Allāh and worship Him Alone) and do not soil their belief with oppression (wrong i.e. by worshipping others besides Allāh), will have security and they are the guided ones." [6:82]

وَعَنْ عُبَادَةَ بْنِ الصَّامِتِ رَضِيَ اللَّهُ عَنْهُ قَالَ: قَالَ رَسُولُ اللهِ صَلَّى اللَّهُ عَلَيْهِ وَسَلَّمَ: «مَنْ شَهِدَ أَنْ لَا إِلَهَ إِلَّا اللهُ، وَحْدَهُ لَا شَرِيكَ لَهُ، وَأَنَّ مُحَمَّدًا عَبْدُهُ وَرَسُولُهُ، وَأَنَّ عِيسَى عَبْدُ اللهِ وَرَسُولُهُ، وَكَلِمَتُهُ أَلْقَاهَا إِلَى مَرْيَمَ، وَرُوحٌ مِنْهُ، وَالْجَنَّةَ حَقٌّ، وَالنَّارَ حَقٌّ، أَدْخَلَهُ اللهُ الْجَنَّةَ عَلَى مَا كَانَ مِنَ الْعَمَلِ». أَخْرَجَاهُ.

'Ubādah b. As-Ṣāmit (رَضِيَ اللَّهُ عَنْهُ) narrated, that Allāh's Messenger (صَلَّى اللَّهُ عَلَيْهِ وَسَلَّمَ) said: "Whoever testifies that there is none worthy of worship in truth except Allāh, Who is without any partners, and that Muḥammad is His slave and Messenger, and that 'Īsa (Jesus) is the slave of Allāh, His Messenger, and His Word which He bestowed in Maryam and a soul (created) from Him, and that Paradise and Hell-fire are realities, Allāh will enter him into Paradise, no matter what his deeds may be." (Ṣaḥiḥ Al-Bukhārī and Ṣaḥiḥ Muslim) [1]

1 — Al-Bukhārī: (3435), Muslim: (28)

وَلَهُمَا فِي حَدِيْثِ عِتْبَانَ: «فَإِنَّ اللهَ حَرَّمَ عَلَى النَّارِ مَنْ قَالَ: (لَا إِلَهَ إِلَّا اللهُ)؛ يَبْتَغِي بِذَلِكَ وَجْهَ اللهِ».

And in Al-Bukhārī and Muslim[1] the narration of 'Itbān (رَضِيَ اللهُ عَنْهُ) narrated that the Prophet (صَلَّى اللهُ عَلَيْهِ وَسَلَّمَ) said: "Indeed Allāh has forbidden Hell for the person who testifies that: 'There is nothing worthy of worship in truth but Allāh', seeking thereby in it nothing but Allāh's Face."

1 — Al-Bukhārī: (425,1186,5401,6423,6938), Muslim: (1496)

وَعَنْ أَبِي سَعِيدٍ الْخُدْرِيِّ رَضِيَ اللَّهُ عَنْهُ، عَنْ رَسُوْلِ اللهِ صَلَّى اللَّهُ عَلَيْهِ وَسَلَّمَ قَالَ: « قَالَ مُوسَى رَحِمَهُ اللَّهُ: يَا رَبِّ عَلِّمْنِي شَيْئًا أَذْكُرُكَ وَأَدْعُوكَ بِهِ، قَالَ: قُلْ يَا مُوسَى: لَا إِلَهَ إِلَّا اللهُ، قَالَ: كُلُّ عِبَادِكَ يَقُولُونَ هَذَا؟ قَالَ: يَا مُوسَى؛ لَوْ أَنَّ السَّمَاوَاتِ السَّبْعَ وَعَامِرَهُنَّ - غَيْرِي - وَالْأَرْضِينَ السَّبْعَ فِي كِفَّةٍ، وَلَا إِلَهَ إِلَّا اللهُ فِي كِفَّةٍ، مَالَتْ بِهِنَّ لَا إِلَهَ إِلَّا اللهُ». رَوَاهُ ابْنُ حِبَّانَ وَالْحَاكِمُ وَصَحَّحَهُ.

Abū Sa'īd Al-Khudrī (رضي الله عنه) narrated that Allāh's Messenger (صلى الله عليه وسلم) said: "Mūsā (Moses) (صلى الله عليه وسلم) said: 'O my Lord, teach me something through which I can remember You and supplicate to You.' Allāh answered: 'Say, O Mūsā, *Lā ilāhā illā-Allāh*'. Mūsā said: 'O my Lord, all your slaves say these words'. Allāh said: 'O Mūsā, if the seven heavens and all they contain — other than Me — and the seven earths as well, were all put on one side of a scale and *Lā ilāhā illa-Allāh* was put on the other scale, the latter would outweigh them.'" (This Hadith has been reported by Ibn Ḥibbān, and al-Hākim declared it Ṣaḥiḥ).[1]

1 — The chain (isnad) of this ḥadīth is weak due to the narrator Darrāj Abī as-Samḥ whose narrations from Abī al-Haytham are weak and denounced (*Al-Ilal* of al-Imām Aḥmad (4482), (at-Taqrīb (1824). This ḥadīth comprises of that weakness. However, perhaps a portion of this narration regarding the virtues of at-Tawhīd can be supported by the narration of 'Abdullāh b. 'Amr from the Prophet (صلى الله عليه وسلم) : "...If the seven heavens and seven earths were placed on a scale and *la ilāhā illa Allāh* was placed on another scale it will outweigh them (seven heavens and seven earths)." (*Al-Adab Al-Mufrad*: (548) with an authentic chain [authenticated by Sh. Al-Albānī (*Ṣaḥīḥ al-Adab al-Mufrad*: 548[426]).

وَلِلتِّرْمِذِيِّ - وَحَسَّنَهُ - عَنْ أَنَسٍ، سَمِعْتُ رَسُولَ اللهِ صَلَّى ٱللَّهُ عَلَيْهِ وَسَلَّمَ يَقُولُ: «قَالَ اللهُ تَعَالَى: يَا ابْنَ آدَمَ، إِنَّكَ لَوْ أَتَيْتَنِي بِقُرَابِ الأَرْضِ خَطَايَا، ثُمَّ لَقِيتَنِي لَا تُشْرِكُ بِي شَيْئًا، لأَتَيْتُكَ بِقُرَابِهَا مَغْفِرَةً».

At-Tirmidhī, who declared this narration as sound, reports from Anas (رَضِيَ ٱللَّهُ عَنْهُ) that he heard Allāh's Messenger (صَلَّى ٱللَّهُ عَلَيْهِ وَسَلَّمَ) say: "Allāh the Most Exalted said: 'O son of Ādam, were you to come to Me with sins that equate to the size of the world, and you meet Me without associating partners with Me (Shirk), I will come to you with a similar amount of forgiveness.'"[1]

1 — At-Tirmidhī : (3540) Aḥmad (35/375). Graded authentic by Sh. Al-Albānī [*Silsilah Ṣaḥiḥah*: 1/199 no. 127) [al-ḥadīth al-Qudsī]

ISSUES OF THIS CHAPTER:

1. The abundance of Allāh's favor.

2. The abundant reward of Tawḥīd towards Allāh.

3. Besides earning rewards, Tawḥīd recompenses sins.

4. Explanation of verse 82 in Surat Al-'An'am.

5. Ponder the five points mentioned in the Ḥadīth narrated by 'Ubādah b. Aṣ-Ṣamit (رَضِيَ ٱللَّهُ عَنْهُ).

6. If you look at the AḤadīth from 'Ubādah and 'Itban (رَضِيَ ٱللَّهُ عَنْهُ) and what follows altogether, the meanings of La-ilaha illa Allāh become clear to you along with the error of those who are the deceived ones (Al-Maghrurīn).

7. Take note of the condition in Itban's Ḥadīth.

8. That the Prophets (صَلَّى ٱللَّهُ عَلَيْهِ وَسَلَّمَ) needed to be apprised of the tremendous virtue of *La ilaha illa-Allāh.*

9. The point of the outweighing of the Kalimah to all other creation, though many who enunciate it will not get the full weight in their balance.

10. The text showing that there are seven earths like seven heavens.

11. That the seven earths and heavens are full of creatures.

12. Confirmation of the Allāh's Attributes, contrary to the claims of Ash'ariyah.

13. Undoubtedly, if you understand the Ḥadīth of Anas (رَضِيَ ٱللَّهُ عَنْهُ), you would understand the statement in the Ḥadīth of Itban (رَضِيَ ٱللَّهُ عَنْهُ):

> "Indeed Allāh has forbidden Hellfire for the person who testifies: 'There is nothing worthy of worship in truth (no true God) except Allāh,' seeking thereby nothing but Allāh's Face."

14. That it constitutes abandonment of Shirk practically and not merely professing *Lā-ilāha illā-Allāh* by the tongue.

15. Reflection and consideration of the shared characteristics of Muḥammad (صَلَّى ٱللَّهُ عَلَيْهِ وَسَلَّمَ) and Īsā (صَلَّى ٱللَّهُ عَلَيْهِ وَسَلَّمَ) both as Prophets and slaves of Allāh.

16. Knowing the peculiarity of Jesus (May Allāh be pleased with him) being created as Kalimat-Allāh (the Word of Allāh).

ISSUES OF THIS CHAPTER:

17. The knowledge that Jesus (صَلَّى ٱللَّهُ عَلَيْهِ وَسَلَّمَ) is a spirit from Allāh (Ruhan Minhu).
18. Knowing the merits of belief in Paradise and Hell.
19. Knowledge of the meaning of the statement of the Prophet (صَلَّى ٱللَّهُ عَلَيْهِ وَسَلَّمَ) "...Whatever his deeds might be."
20. The knowledge that Al-Mīzān (the Scale) consists of two sides.
21. What is meant by the mention of the "Face" (of Allāh).

CHAPTER EXERCISES

1. What is the meaning of Allāh's statement "...and that Īsā is His slave and Messenger"? Who is this a refutation on?
2. Mention three virtues of at-Tawhīd.
3. What is the meaning of the testimony *'lā ilāhā illa Allāh'*?
4. What does "...and that Muḥammad (صَلَّى ٱللَّهُ عَلَيْهِ وَسَلَّمَ) is His slave and Messenger" mean? What does this necessitate?
5. What is the suitability of the narration of 'Ubādah to this chapter?

CHAPTER EXERCISES

CHAPTER EXERCISES

CHAPTER 2:

Whoever Establishes at-Tawhīd Enters Paradise without Being Taken to Account

وَقَوْلِ اللهِ تَعَالَى: «إِنَّ إِبْرَاهِيمَ كَانَ أُمَّةً قَانِتًا لِّلَّهِ حَنِيفًا وَلَمْ يَكُ مِنَ الْمُشْرِكِينَ» النحل: ١٢٠

Allāh the Most Exalted said: "Verily Ibrāhīm was a nation (ummah), devoutly obedient to Allāh, unswervingly true in faith and he was not of those who ascribed partners to Allāh." [16: 120]

وقال: «وَالَّذِينَ هُم بِرَبِّهِمْ لَا يُشْرِكُونَ» المؤمنون ٥٩

And He said: "And those who ascribe not anyone (in worship) as partners with their Lord." [23:59]

وَعَنْ حُصَيْنِ بْنِ عَبْدِ الرَّحْمَنِ قَالَ: كُنْتُ عِنْدَ سَعِيدِ بْنِ جُبَيْرٍ، فَقَالَ: أَيُّكُمْ رَأَى الْكَوْكَبَ الَّذِي انْقَضَّ الْبَارِحَةَ؟ فَقُلْتُ: أَنَا، ثُمَّ قُلْتُ: أَمَا إِنِّي لَمْ أَكُنْ فِي صَلَاةٍ؛ وَلَكِنِّي لُدِغْتُ، قَالَ: فَمَا صَنَعْتَ؟ قُلْتُ: ارْتَقَيْتُ، قَالَ: فَمَا حَمَلَكَ عَلَى ذَلِكَ؟ قُلْتُ: حَدِيثٌ حَدَّثَنَاهُ الشَّعْبِيُّ، قَالَ: وَمَا حَدَّثَكُمْ؟ قُلْتُ: حَدَّثَنَا عَنْ بُرَيْدَةَ بْنِ الْحُصَيْبِ؛ أَنَّهُ قَالَ: «لَا رُقْيَةَ إِلَّا مِنْ عَيْنٍ أَوْ حُمَةٍ»،

Ḥuṣain b. 'Abdur-Raḥmān narrated: Once when I was with Sa'īd b. Jubair, he asked, "Who from you saw the shooting star last night?" I answered, "I saw it," and then explained that I was not in prayer at the time rather I had been stung by a poisonous scorpion. He said, "What did you do then?" I replied, "I used Ruqyah to cure it!" He said, "What compelled you to do that?" I said, "A narration I heard from ash-Sh'abī." He asked, "What did ash-Sh'abī narrate?" I replied, "He reported from Buraidah b. al-Ḥuṣaib, who said that Ruqyah is not allowed except for the treatment of 'evil eye' and (poisonous) stings..."

قالَ: قَدْ أَحْسَنَ مَنِ انْتَهَى إِلَى مَا سَمِعَ؛ وَلَكِنْ حَدَّثَنَا ابْنُ عَبَّاسٍ ، عَنِ النَّبِيِّ أَنَّهُ قَالَ: «عُرِضَتْ عَلَيَّ الأُمَمُ، فَرَأَيْتُ النَّبِيَّ وَمَعَهُ الرَّهْطُ، وَالنَّبِيَّ وَمَعَهُ الرَّجُلُ وَالرَّجُلَانِ، وَالنَّبِيَّ وَلَيْسَ مَعَهُ أَحَدٌ، إِذْ رُفِعَ لِي سَوَادٌ عَظِيمٌ، فَظَنَنْتُ أَنَّهُمْ أُمَّتِي، فَقِيلَ لِي: هَذَا مُوسَى وَقَوْمُهُ، فَنَظَرْتُ فَإِذَا سَوَادٌ عَظِيمٌ، فَقِيلَ لِي: هَذِهِ أُمَّتُكَ، وَمَعَهُمْ سَبْعُونَ أَلْفًا يَدْخُلُونَ الْجَنَّةَ بِغَيْرِ حِسَابٍ وَلَا عَذَابٍ»

He (Sa'īd bin Jubair) said, "He has done well by stopping on what he has heard (i.e. to act according to the knowledge as opposed to ignorance). However, Ibn 'Abbās (رَضِيَ اللَّهُ عَنْهُمَا) narrated to us that the Prophet (صَلَّى اللَّهُ عَلَيْهِ وَسَلَّمَ) said, 'All the nations were made to pass before me, and I saw a Prophet with a small group with him, and a Prophet with two or three people and a Prophet with none. Then there appeared a large group of people which I took to be my nation (Ummah). But I was told that they were Mūsā and his people. Later, a larger group appeared and I was told that they were my people. Among them were seventy thousand who would enter Paradise without reckoning or punishment.'

ثُمَّ نَهَضَ فَدَخَلَ مَنْزِلَهُ، فَخَاضَ النَّاسُ فِي أُولَئِكَ، فَقَالَ بَعْضُهُمْ: فَلَعَلَّهُمُ الَّذِينَ صَحِبُوا رَسُوْلَ اللهِ ، وَقَالَ بَعْضُهُمْ: فَلَعَلَّهُمُ الَّذِينَ وُلِدُوا فِي الإِسْلَامِ فَلَمْ يُشْرِكُوا بِاللهِ شَيْئًا، وَذَكَرُوا أَشْيَاءَ، فَخَرَجَ عَلَيْهِمْ رَسُوْلُ اللهِ فَأَخْبَرُوهُ، فَقَالَ: «هُمُ الَّذِينَ لَا يَسْتَرْقُونَ، وَلَا يَكْتَوُونَ، وَلَا يَتَطَيَّرُونَ، وَعَلَى رَبِّهِمْ يَتَوَكَّلُونَ»، فَقَامَ عُكَّاشَةُ بْنُ مِحْصَنٍ؛ فَقَالَ: يَا رَسُوْلَ اللهِ، ادْعُ اللهَ أَنْ يَجْعَلَنِي مِنْهُمْ، فَقَالَ: «أَنْتَ مِنْهُمْ»، ثُمَّ قَامَ رَجُلٌ آخَرُ، فَقَالَ: ادْعُ اللهَ أَنْ يَجْعَلَنِي مِنْهُمْ، فَقَالَ: «سَبَقَكَ بِهَا عُكَّاشَةُ».

The Prophet (ﷺ) then got up and went into his house, and the people went into a discussion as to who they might be. Some said, 'Perhaps they are the Companions of the Messenger of Allāh (ﷺ).' Others said, 'Maybe they are those who were born in Islam and therefore never ascribed partners with Allāh.' Whilst they were exchanging their views, the Prophet (ﷺ) came out and was informed about the discussion. He said, they are those who do not request others to perform Ruqyah on them, nor do they believe in omens or do they cauterize themselves, but rather they put their trust in their Lord.' On that, 'Ukāshah b. Miḥṣan (رَضِيَ ٱللَّهُ عَنْهُ) rose and said to the Prophet (ﷺ) 'Invoke Allāh to make me one of them.' He (ﷺ) said, 'You are one of them.' Then another man got up and said, 'Invoke Allāh to make me one of them.' He (ﷺ) said, 'Ukāshah has preceded you.'"[1]

1 — Al-Bukhārī: (5705), Muslim (220) the wording is specifically from Ṣaḥīḥ Muslim.

ISSUES OF THIS CHAPTER:

1. Regarding Tawḥīd, people are classified into various ranks.
2. The meaning of 'purification of Tawḥīd'.
3. Ibrāhim (صَلَّى ٱللَّهُ عَلَيْهِ وَسَلَّمَ) was praised by Allāh for he was not of the polytheists.
4. Allāh praised all those Auliya for they did not make anyone with Him as the partner (did not practice polytheism).
5. Keeping away from cauterization and Ruqyah is the fullest purification of Tawḥīd.
6. Possessing these characteristics (traits) is from at-Tawakkul (trusting in Allāh Alone).
7. The deep knowledge of the Companions of Prophet Muḥammad (صَلَّى ٱللَّهُ عَلَيْهِ وَسَلَّمَ) who knew that such a degree of trust (Tawakkul) in Allāh could not be attained without action.
8. This shows how eager the Companions were in doing good deeds.
9. The superiority of the followers of Muḥammad (صَلَّى ٱللَّهُ عَلَيْهِ وَسَلَّمَ) quantitatively as well as qualitatively.
10. The superiority of the Ummah (followers) of Musā (صَلَّى ٱللَّهُ عَلَيْهِ وَسَلَّمَ).
11. All the Ummam (nations) will be paraded before the Prophet Muḥammad (صَلَّى ٱللَّهُ عَلَيْهِ وَسَلَّمَ).
12. Every Ummah (nation) will be accompanied by its respective Prophet.
13. Generally, few people responded to the call of the Prophets.
14. The Prophets, whom nobody responded to, will come alone before Allāh.
15. The substance of these facts is that man should not worry about numbers, neither must he feel proud about huge numbers nor be disheartened by fewer numbers.
16. The permission for using Ruqyah to treat the evil eye and poisonous stings.
17. By the Ḥadīth "He has done well by stopping by what he has heard", the depth of knowledge of the predecessors is known, and it is also known that the first Ḥadīth does not contradict the second.
18. The avoidance of the predecessors in praising anyone undeservedly.

ISSUES OF THIS CHAPTER:

19. The Prophet's (صَلَّى ٱللَّهُ عَلَيْهِ وَسَلَّمَ) statement that 'You are one of them' is a sign of Prophethood.

20. The excellence of Ukkashah (رَضِيَ ٱللَّهُ عَنْهُ).

21. Using Ma'areed (to mention something casually among other things, or a description open to various interpretations).

22. The excellent manners of Prophet Muḥammad (صَلَّى ٱللَّهُ عَلَيْهِ وَسَلَّمَ).

CHAPTER EXERCISES

1. Name three characteristics of Ibrāhīm (صَلَّى ٱللَّهُ عَلَيْهِ وَسَلَّمَ).
2. Name two virtues of at-Tawhīd taken from this chapter.
3. From the ḥadīth of Ḥuṣain b. 'Abdur-Raḥmān, give an example of an act of sincerity.
4. Why does belief in omens contradict at-Tawḥīd?
5. What is the appropriateness of the ḥadīth of Ḥuṣain b. 'Abdur-Raḥmān to the chapter heading?

CHAPTER EXERCISES

CHAPTER EXERCISES

CHAPTER 3:

The Fear of Falling into Shirk

> وَقَوْلِ اللهِ تَعَالَى: ﴿إِنَّ اللَّهَ لَا يَغْفِرُ أَن يُشْرَكَ بِهِ وَيَغْفِرُ مَا دُونَ ذَٰلِكَ لِمَن يَشَاءُ﴾ النساء: ٤٨
>
> "Verily, Allāh does not forgive that partners be associated with Him in worship, but He forgives other than that to whom He pleases." [4:48, 116]

> وَقال الخليل: ﴿وَاجْنُبْنِي وَبَنِيَّ أَن نَّعْبُدَ الْأَصْنَامَ﴾ إبراهيم: ٣٥
>
> Allāh stated that Ibrāhīm said: "And keep me and my sons away from worshipping idols." [14:35]

وَفِي الحَدِيثِ: « أَخْوَفُ مَا أَخَافُ عَلَيْكُمْ: الشِّرْكُ الأَصْغَرُ، فَسُئِلَ عَنْهُ؟ فَقَالَ: الرِّيَاءُ.»

" It is narrated in the ḥadīth : "What I fear most for you is a minor form of Shirk." When asked about it, he said, "Ar-Riyāa (showing off)." [1]

1 — Narrated by Maḥmūd b. Labīd: At-Ṭabarānī in *al-Kabīr* (4310) and *al-Sh'uab* (6412). Declared very sound by Al-Mundhirī (At-Targhīb wa at-Tarhīb: 1/69) and Sh. Al-Albānī (*as-Ṣaḥiḥah*: 951).

وَعَنِ ابْنِ مَسْعُودٍ ﷺ؛ أَنَّ رَسُولَ اللهِ ﷺ قَالَ: «مَنْ مَاتَ وَهُوَ يَدْعُو للهِ نِدًّا؛ دَخَلَ النَّارَ». رَوَاهُ الْبُخَارِيُّ.

Ibn Mas'ūd (رَضِيَ اللَّهُ عَنْهُ) narrated that Prophet Muḥammad (صَلَّى اللَّهُ عَلَيْهِ وَسَلَّمَ)said: "Whoever dies while associating partners with Allāh, enters the Hellfire." (Al-Bukhārī) [1]

1 — Al-Bukhārī: (4497)

وَلِمُسْلِمٍ عَنْ جَابِرٍ رضي الله عنه؛ أَنَّ رَسُولَ اللهِ ﷺ قَالَ: «مَنْ لَقِيَ اللهَ لَا يُشْرِكُ بِهِ شَيْئًا دَخَلَ الْجَنَّةَ، وَمَنْ لَقِيَهُ يُشْرِكُ بِهِ شَيْئًا دَخَلَ النَّارَ.»

Muslim[1] reports from Jābir (رضي الله عنه) that Allāh's Messenger (صلى الله عليه وسلم) said: "Whoever meets Allāh (on the Day of Judgement) not having associated anyone with Him (in worship), shall enter Paradise; and whoever meets Him having committed Shirk in any way will enter the Hellfire."

1 — Ḥadīth Number (93 and 152)

ISSUES OF THIS CHAPTER:

1. Fear of Shirk (polytheism).

2. Showing off (Riyaa) is a type of Shirk.

3. Showing off is a lesser type of Shirk.

4. Falling into minor Shirk (Riyaa) is more fearful to the righteous and pious people than any other matter.

5. The nearness of Paradise and Hell.

6. Combination of the nearness of Paradise and Hell has been stated in the same ḥadīth.

7. Whoever meets Allāh having associated nothing with Him, shall enter Paradise; and whoever dies while committing Shirk with Allāh in any way shall enter Hell, even though he might have been an ardent worshipper.

8. The important issue of the invocation of Ibrāhīm (صَلَّى ٱللَّهُ عَلَيْهِ وَسَلَّمَ) for himself and his progeny, being the protection from the worship of idols.

9. The acknowledgment of Ibrāhīm (صَلَّى ٱللَّهُ عَلَيْهِ وَسَلَّمَ) of the condition of most people that "O my Lord, they have indeed led astray many from mankind."

10. An explanation of the meaning of (the Kalimah) "Nothing is deserving of worship in truth besides Allāh" as reported by Al- Bukhārī.

11. The superiority of one who is free from Shirk.

CHAPTER EXERCISES

1. Name one ill effect of associating partners with Allāh in worship.
2. What is the significance of Ibrāhīm's supplication to Allāh?
3. What is the evidence that the one that falls into a major sin is not taken out of the fold of Islām?
4. Mention a proof from this chapter for the belief in the Hereafter.
5. What are the main categories of shirk?

CHAPTER EXERCISES

CHAPTER 4:

The Call to the Testification that None Deserves to be Worshiped in Except Allāh

وَقَوْلِ اللهِ تَعَالَى: « قُلْ هَٰذِهِ سَبِيلِي أَدْعُو إِلَى اللَّهِ ۚ عَلَىٰ بَصِيرَةٍ أَنَا وَمَنِ اتَّبَعَنِي ۖ وَسُبْحَانَ اللَّهِ وَمَا أَنَا مِنَ الْمُشْرِكِينَ « يوسف: ١٠٨

Allāh the Exalted said: "Say (O Muḥammad ﷺ): 'This is my way; I call to Allāh with sure knowledge, I and whosoever follows me. And Glorified and Exalted is Allāh I am not from the polytheists.'" [12: 108]

عَنِ ابْنِ عَبَّاسٍ رَضِيَ ٱللَّهُ عَنْهُمَا أَنَّ رَسُولَ اللهِ صَلَّى ٱللَّهُ عَلَيْهِ وَسَلَّمَ لَمَّا بَعَثَ مُعَاذًا إِلَى الْيَمَنِ قَالَ لَهُ: «إِنَّكَ تَأْتِي قَوْمًا مِنْ أَهْلِ الْكِتَابِ، فَلْيَكُنْ أَوَّلَ مَا تَدْعُوهُمْ إِلَيْهِ شَهَادَةُ أَنْ لَا إِلَهَ إِلَّا اللهُ – وَفِي رِوَايَةٍ: إِلَى أَنْ يُوَحِّدُوا اللهَ – فَإِنْ هُمْ أَطَاعُوكَ لِذَلِكَ؛ فَأَعْلِمْهُمْ أَنَّ اللهَ افْتَرَضَ عَلَيْهِمْ خَمْسَ صَلَوَاتٍ فِي كُلِّ يَوْمٍ وَلَيْلَةٍ،

Ibn 'Abbās (رَضِيَ ٱللَّهُ عَنْهُمَا) narrated: When Allāh's Messenger (صَلَّى ٱللَّهُ عَلَيْهِ وَسَلَّمَ) sent Mu'ādh (رَضِيَ ٱللَّهُ عَنْهُ) to Yemen, he said, "You will come upon the People of the Book, let your first act be to call them to testify that — there is nothing worthy of worship in truth but Allāh." And in another wording of this hadeeth: "To single out Allāh Alone in the worship. If they obey you in this, inform them that Allāh has prescribed five prayers every day and night...

فَإِنْ هُمْ أَطَاعُوكَ لِذَلِكَ، فَأَعْلِمْهُمْ أَنَّ اللهَ افْتَرَضَ عَلَيْهِمْ صَدَقَةً تُؤْخَذُ مِنْ أَغْنِيَائِهِمْ فَتُرَدُّ عَلَى فُقَرَائِهِمْ، فَإِنْ هُمْ أَطَاعُوكَ لِذَلِكَ، فَإِيَّاكَ وَكَرَائِمَ أَمْوَالِهِمْ، وَاتَّقِ دَعْوَةَ الْمَظْلُومِ؛ فَإِنَّهُ لَيْسَ بَيْنَهَا وَبَيْنَ اللهِ حِجَابٌ». أَخْرَجَاهُ.

If they obey you in this, then inform them that Allāh has made obligatory upon them the duty of paying Sadaqah (Zakat). This is to be taken from their rich and distributed to the poor. If they obey you in this, then be careful not to take the best part of their wealth (as payment of Zakat), and safeguard yourself against the supplication of the oppressed one as there is no veil between his supplication and Allāh."[1]

1 — Al-Bukhārī: (1395,1496,4347) and Muslim: (19)

> وَلَهُمَا عَنْ سَهْلِ بْنِ سَعْدٍ رَضِيَ ٱللَّهُ عَنْهُ؛ أَنَّ رَسُولَ اللهِ صَلَّى ٱللَّهُ عَلَيْهِ وَسَلَّمَ قَالَ يَوْمَ خَيْبَرَ: «لأُعْطِيَنَّ الرَّايَةَ غَدًا رَجُلًا يُحِبُّ اللهَ وَرَسُولَهُ، وَيُحِبُّهُ اللهُ وَرَسُولُهُ، يَفْتَحُ اللهُ عَلَى يَدَيْهِ»، فَبَاتَ النَّاسُ يَدُوكُونَ لَيْلَتَهُمْ، أَيُّهُمْ يُعْطَاهَا، فَلَمَّا أَصْبَحُوا غَدَوْا عَلَى رَسُولِ اللهِ صَلَّى ٱللَّهُ عَلَيْهِ وَسَلَّمَ، كُلُّهُمْ يَرْجُو أَنْ يُعْطَاهَا،
>
> Both collectors have also reported[1] that Sahl b. Sa'd (رَضِيَ ٱللَّهُ عَنْهُ) said: On the day of Khaybar, Allāh's Messenger (صَلَّى ٱللَّهُ عَلَيْهِ وَسَلَّمَ) said, "Tomorrow I shall give the flag to a person who loves Allāh and His Messenger (صَلَّى ٱللَّهُ عَلَيْهِ وَسَلَّمَ) and is loved by Allāh and His Messenger (صَلَّى ٱللَّهُ عَلَيْهِ وَسَلَّمَ). Allāh will grant victory under his leadership." The people spent the night absorbed in discussing as to whom might the flag be given to! In the morning they came eagerly to Allāh's Messenger (صَلَّى ٱللَّهُ عَلَيْهِ وَسَلَّمَ), each of them hoping to be given the flag...

1 — Al-Bukhārī: (2942) and Muslim: (2406)

فَقَالَ: «أَيْنَ عَلِيُّ بْنُ أَبِي طَالِبٍ؟»، فَقِيلَ: هُوَ يَشْتَكِي عَيْنَيْهِ، فَأَرْسَلُوا إِلَيْهِ فَأُتِيَ بِهِ، فَبَصَقَ فِي عَيْنَيْهِ وَدَعَا لَهُ؛ فَبَرَأَ كَأَنْ لَمْ يَكُنْ بِهِ وَجَعٌ، فَأَعْطَاهُ الرَّايَةَ، فَقَالَ: «انفُذْ عَلَى رِسْلِكَ حَتَّى تَنْزِلَ بِسَاحَتِهِمْ، ثُمَّ ادْعُهُمْ إِلَى الإِسْلَامِ، وَأَخْبِرْهُمْ بِمَا يَجِبُ عَلَيْهِمْ مِنْ حَقِّ اللهِ تَعَالَى فِيهِ، فَوَاللهِ لَأَنْ يَهْدِيَ اللهُ بِكَ رَجُلًا وَاحِدًا خَيْرٌ لَكَ مِنْ حُمْرِ النَّعَمِ.» {يَدُوكُونَ} أَيْ يَخُوضُونَ.

Allāh's Messenger (صَلَّىٰٱللَّهُعَلَيۡهِوَسَلَّمَ) asked, "Where is 'Ali b. Abī Ṭālib (رَضِيَٱللَّهُعَنۡهُ)?" They replied, "He is suffering from an eye ailment." He was sent for and brought. Allāh's Messenger (صَلَّىٰٱللَّهُعَلَيۡهِوَسَلَّمَ) then spat in his eyes and prayed for him, whereupon he was cured as if he did not have any ailments. Allāh's Messenger (صَلَّىٰٱللَّهُعَلَيۡهِوَسَلَّمَ) then gave him the flag and said, "Go gently and steadily until you arrive in their midst, then call them to Islām and inform them of their duties to Allāh the Exalted. By Allāh, that he guides through you a single man is better for you than red camels."[1]

1 — Al-Bukhārī: (3701, 4210 with a slightly different wording) Muslim: (2406)

ISSUES OF THIS CHAPTER:

1. It is the way of the followers of Prophet Muḥammad (صَلَّى ٱللَّهُ عَلَيْهِ وَسَلَّمَ) to call people to Islam.
2. Stress upon the sincerity of intention, for many who supposedly call to the truth merely call to themselves.
3. Calling people to Allāh with sure knowledge is obligatory.
4. Of the signs of the beauty of Tawḥīd is it's being free of any blasphemy towards Allāh.
5. The ugliness of Shirk is that it vilifies Allāh.
6. Of the most important Issues of this Chapter is that a Muslim must and should remain aloof from polytheists to not become like them even if he does not himself commit Shirk.
7. Implementing Tawḥīd (and calling to it) is the foremost obligation.
8. We must first begin with Tawḥīd before anything else, even before the prayer.
9. The meaning of singling out Allāh Alone in worship and being sincere in His Oneness is the meaning of the testification; "Lā ilāha illa-Allāh ".
10. From the people of the Scriptures are some who either have no knowledge of Tawḥīd or if they do, they don't adhere to.
11. Stress on teaching step by step.
12. The most important issues must be explained first.
13. How to spend Zakat (obligatory charity).
14. The scholar clarifying misconceptions for the student.
15. The prohibition on taking the best part of the people's wealth in charity.
16. Beware of the supplication of the oppressed.
17. We are informed that there is no barrier to the supplication of the oppressed (it is accepted).

ISSUES OF THIS CHAPTER:

18. The afflictions, hardship, hunger, and epidemics suffered by the head of all the Prophets and the best of those close to Allāh (صَلَّى ٱللَّهُ عَلَيْهِ وَسَلَّمَ) are nothing but pieces of evidence of Tawḥīd.

19. The Prophet's assertion: "I shall indeed give the flag ..." is a sign from among the signs of Prophethood.

20. Applying spit to the eyes of 'Ali (رَضِيَ ٱللَّهُ عَنْهُ) and the subsequent cure he received, is another sign of the Prophethood of Muḥammad (صَلَّى ٱللَّهُ عَلَيْهِ وَسَلَّمَ).

21. The superiority of 'Ali (رَضِيَ ٱللَّهُ عَنْهُ).

22. The merits and virtues of the Companions (رَضِيَ ٱللَّهُ عَنْهُمْ) that they kept speculating among themselves throughout the night (as to whom the flag might be handed over to) and their preoccupation ahead of the news of lasting victory (in battle).

23. An illustration of the belief in Qadar — how the predetermined occurs to those who do not seek it and denial to those who wished it all along the night.

24. The manner of the Prophet's (صَلَّى ٱللَّهُ عَلَيْهِ وَسَلَّمَ) advice to Alī (رَضِيَ ٱللَّهُ عَنْهُ) "Go to the people with ease and gentleness."

25. Calling to Islam before waging war.

26. The legitimacy of fighting with those who were previously called to Islam but rejected it.

27. Preaching Islam with wisdom as evidenced in his (صَلَّى ٱللَّهُ عَلَيْهِ وَسَلَّمَ) words: "Inform them of the obligations upon them."

28. Recognizing the rights of Allāh in Islam.

29. The reward of a person by whose hand a single man is guided.

30. To swear in support of a juristic verdict.

CHAPTER EXERCISES

1. What is the proof in this chapter of the correct methodology in calling (da'wah) to Allāh? Explain.

2. Mention a sign from the signs of the prophethood of Muḥammad (صَلَّى ٱللَّهُ عَلَيْهِ وَسَلَّمَ).

3. From this chapter, name one virtue of calling to Allāh.

4. Mention three specific benefits from the ḥadīth of Mu'ādh b. Jabal (رَضِيَ ٱللَّهُ عَنْهُ).

5. Mention two places in this chapter where the importance of seeking knowledge is highlighted.

CHAPTER EXERCISES

CHAPTER EXERCISES

CHAPTER 5:

The Explanation of Tawhid and The Testimony of *Lā ilāhā illā Allāh*

وَقَوْلِ اللهِ تَعَالَى: « أُولَٰئِكَ الَّذِينَ يَدْعُونَ يَبْتَغُونَ إِلَىٰ رَبِّهِمُ الْوَسِيلَةَ أَيُّهُمْ أَقْرَبُ وَيَرْجُونَ رَحْمَتَهُ وَيَخَافُونَ عَذَابَهُ ۚ إِنَّ عَذَابَ رَبِّكَ كَانَ مَحْذُورًا » الإسراء: ٥٧

Allāh the Almighty said: "Those whom they call upon desire (for themselves) a means of getting close to their Lord (Allāh), competing as to whom will be nearest to Him whilst hoping for His Mercy and fearing His Torment. Verily; the Torment of Your Lord is something to be afraid of." [17:57]

وَقَوْله «وَإِذْ قَالَ إِبْرَاهِيمُ لِأَبِيهِ وَقَوْمِهِ إِنَّنِي بَرَاءٌ مِّمَّا تَعْبُدُونَ ۝ إِلَّا الَّذِي فَطَرَنِي فَإِنَّهُ سَيَهْدِينِ » الزخرف: ٢٦ - ٢٧

He also said: "And when Ibrāhīm said to his father and people; Indeed, I am free from that which you worship other than the one (Allāh) who created me." [43:27-28]

وَقَوْلُهُ: «اتَّخَذُوا أَحْبَارَهُمْ وَرُهْبَانَهُمْ أَرْبَابًا مِّن دُونِ اللَّهِ.» التوبة: ٣١

Allāh the Almighty said: "They (Jews and Christians) took their rabbis and monks as lords besides Allāh." [9:31]

> وقَوْلُهُ: «وَمِنَ النَّاسِ مَن يَتَّخِذُ مِن دُونِ اللَّهِ أَندَادًا يُحِبُّونَهُمْ كَحُبِّ اللَّهِ » البقرة: ١٦٥
>
> He said: "And from mankind are those who take others as rivals with Allāh. They love them as they love Allāh." [2: 165]

وَفِي الصَّحِيحِ عَنِ النَّبِيِّ صَلَّى اللَّهُ عَلَيْهِ وَسَلَّمَ أَنَّهُ قَالَ: «مَنْ قَالَ: لَا إِلَهَ إِلَّا اللهُ وَكَفَرَ بِمَا يُعْبَدُ مِنْ دُونِ اللهِ؛ حَرُمَ مَالُهُ وَدَمُهُ، وَحِسَابُهُ عَلَى اللهِ عَزَّ وَجَلَّ.»

And in the *Ṣaḥiḥ*[1], it is reported that the Prophet (صَلَّى اللَّهُ عَلَيْهِ وَسَلَّمَ) said: "He who professed that there is no deity to be worshipped but Allāh and made a denial of everything which the people worship besides Allāh, his property and blood become inviolable, and his affair rests with Allāh."

The remaining chapters of this book are explanations of this chapter.

---

1 — Muslim: (23) from the narration of Abī Mālik whose father Ṭāriq b. Ashyam (رَضِيَ اللَّهُ عَنْهُ) relayed it to him.

ISSUES OF THIS CHAPTER:

This chapter contains the greatest and most important of issues namely the explanation of Tawḥīd and the testimony of Faith and clarification of it through clear matters.

Of these matters is the verse in Surah Al-Isrā'. It is a clear refutation of the polytheists who supplicate the righteous ones as well as making clear that to do so is major Shirk.

Also the verse in Surah Al-Barā'ah clearly shows that the People of the Book took their priests and their rabbis as lords besides Allāh. It is also clear that they were not ordered except to worship a single deity (i.e. Allāh). The explanation of the Verse which has no ambiguity in their obedience to the scholars and other slaves of Allāh in sinful things and not calling or supplicating them.

Additionally is the statement of Ibrāhīm (Peace be upon him) to the disbelievers wherein he excepted his Lord from other deities:

> "Verily, I am innocent of what you worship except Him, Who did create created me."(42:26, 27)

Allāh mentioned that this being free from Shirk explains the testimony of La ilaha illa-Allāh, for He said:

> "And He made it [i.e. La ilaha illa-Allāh (none has the right to be worshipped but Allāh Alone)] a Word lasting among his offspring that they may turn back." (43:28)

There is the verse of Surah Al-Baqarah regarding the disbelievers where Allāh said of them:

> "They will not get out of the Fire" (2:167)

It is mentioned that they love those whom they associate with Allāh, as they love Allāh, and this points to the fact that they do indeed love Allāh tremendously but this nevertheless did not bring them into the fold of Islam. Then how about the one who loves the false deity more than he loves Allāh? How about the one who loves none other than his false deity and has no love for Allāh?

ISSUES OF THIS CHAPTER:

The Prophet (صَلَّىٰ ٱللَّهُ عَلَيْهِ وَسَلَّمَ) stated:

> "Whoever says La ilaha illa-Allāh and rejects all other things that are worshipped besides Allāh, his wealth and his blood are inviolable and his account rests with Allāh."

This is from the weightiest statements clarifying the meaning of La ilaha illa-Allāh. It shows that a mere pronouncement does not protect the pronouncer's blood and wealth. It is insufficient to simply understand its evident meaning and words, to acknowledge it, or even to call on none other than Allāh, Who is Alone and without partners. Rather, the pronouncer's wealth and blood do not become inviolable until, in addition to all of the above, he fully rejects all that is falsely worshipped besides Allāh. If anyone has doubt or hesitates in this, neither his wealth nor blood is safe. What greater or more splendid an example can be given? What could elucidate the point more clearly? What more conclusive of an argument is there to cut off any dispute in the matter?

CHAPTER EXERCISES

1. Which of the five necessities of life that need preserving are mentioned in this chapter?
2. From this chapter, what is the refutation of those who worship or supplicate to the prophets, angels, and the pious?
3. What are the pillars of "lā ilāhā illa Allāh"? Where are they mentioned in this chapter?
4. Give one explanation of at-Tawḥīd taken from the texts mentioned in this chapter.
5. Where in this chapter is the proof for the pillars of worship?

CHAPTER EXERCISES

CHAPTER EXERCISES

CHAPTER 6:

Wearing a Ring, Twine, and its Likes for Prevention or Lifting of Harm is an Act of Shirk

وقَوْل الله تعالى: «قُلْ أَفَرَأَيْتُم مَّا تَدْعُونَ مِن دُونِ اللَّهِ إِنْ أَرَادَنِيَ اللَّهُ بِضُرٍّ هَلْ هُنَّ كَاشِفَاتُ ضُرِّهِ» الزمر: ٣٨ الآية.

Allāh the Exalted said: "Say: Tell me then, regarding those that you invoke besides Allāh, if Allāh decreed some harm for me, could they remove it?" [39:38]

عَنْ عِمْرَانَ بْنِ حُصَيْنٍ رَضِيَ اللَّهُ عَنْهُ؛ أَنَّ النَّبِيَّ صَلَّى اللَّهُ عَلَيْهِ وَسَلَّمَ رَأَى رَجُلًا فِي يَدِهِ حَلْقَةٌ مِنْ صُفْرٍ، فَقَالَ: «مَا هَذِهِ؟»، قَالَ: مِنَ الْوَاهِنَةِ، فَقَالَ: «انْزِعْهَا؛ فَإِنَّهَا لَا تَزِيدُكَ إِلَّا وَهْنًا، فَإِنَّكَ لَوْ مُتَّ وَهِيَ عَلَيْكَ مَا أَفْلَحْتَ أَبَدًا». رَوَاهُ أَحْمَدُ بِسَنَدٍ لَا بَأْسَ بِهِ.

'Imrān b. Ḥuṣain (رَضِيَ اللَّهُ عَنْهُ) narrated: The Prophet (صَلَّى اللَّهُ عَلَيْهِ وَسَلَّمَ) once saw a man with a brass ring on his hand and asked him, "What is this?" The man replied, "To over-come the weakness of old age." He said, "Remove it, for, it can only add to your weakness. Should death reach you whilst you are wearing it, you would never succeed." [This Hadith was recorded by Aḥmad (b. Ḥanbal) with an acceptable chain of narrators.] [1]

1 — The chain in the Musnad of al-Imām Aḥmad (33/204), ibn Mājah (3135) and others is weak (Da'īf); it has a narrator called Mubārak b. Faḍālah who narrated from Ḥasan al-Baṣrī. However, Mubārak did not explicitly say he heard this particular narration from Ḥasan al-Baṣarī, the mode of transmission was vague. Mubārak is one of those narrators (mudallis) that in order to accept their narrations there must be no vagueness in the mode of transmission as is mentioned by ibn Ḥajr in at-Taqrīb (7474). The mode of transmission here is vague. Imām Aḥmad said that the narrations of Mubārak from Ḥasan al-Baṣarī are accepted and considered (*Tahdhīb at-Tahdhīb:* 10/29). However, this is if it is established that he explicitly heard this specific narration from Ḥasan al-Baṣrī, which is not the case here. In addition, Ḥasan al-Baṣarī did not meet 'Imrān b. Ḥuṣain so this adds further weakness to this ḥadīth as there is a disconnection. See (*al-Marāsīl* of ibn Abī Ḥātim: p.38 no.120,121 and 123) (*aḍ-Ḍa'īfah*: 1029).

The narration is weak (Da'īf),but the meaning is correct. Shaykh al-Islām ibn Taymiyyah mentioned regarding texts such as this" It is not used as a fundamental proof but mentioned along with other fundamental texts that are authentic and free of discrepancies to show that the meaning is correct" (*Ar-Radd 'alā al-Bakrī*: 118). Perhaps this was the reason why the author mentioned this narration and Allāh knows best.

وَلَهُ عَنْ عُقْبَةَ بْنِ عَامِرٍ مَرْفُوعًا: «مَنْ تَعَلَّقَ تَمِيمَةً فَلَا أَتَمَّ اللهُ لَهُ، وَمَنْ تَعَلَّقَ وَدَعَةً فَلَا وَدَعَ اللهُ لَهُ».

وَفِي رِوَايَةٍ: «مَنْ تَعَلَّقَ تَمِيمَةً فَقَدْ أَشْرَكَ».

He also recorded a Marfū'[1] Ḥadīth; 'Uqbah bin Aāmir (رَضِيَ اللَّهُ عَنْهُ): "Whoever wears talisman or an amulet would never see his wish fulfilled by Allāh. And whoever hangs a sea shell would never get peace and rest."[2] In another version; "Whoever wears a talisman has committed Shirk (polytheism)."[3]

---

1 — Lifted and ascribed to the Messenger (صَلَّى اللَّهُ عَلَيْهِ وَسَلَّمَ).

2 — *Musnad* of Imām Aḥmad: (28/623) *At-Targhīb* of al-Mundhirī: (4/306) who said the chain is good.

3 — *Musnad* of Imām Aḥmad: (28/628), Authenticated by Sh. Al-Albānī (*Ṣaḥīḥ at-Targhīb*: 3/348).

وَلِابْنِ أَبِي حَاتِمٍ عَنْ حُذَيْفَةَ؛ أَنَّهُ رَأَى رَجُلًا فِي يَدِهِ خَيْطٌ مِنَ الْحُمَّى، فَقَطَعَهُ، وَتَلَا قَوْلَهُ: « وَمَا يُؤْمِنُ أَكْثَرُهُم بِاللَّهِ إِلَّا وَهُم مُّشْرِكُونَ» يوسف: ١٠٦

Ibn Abī Hātim reported about Ḥudhaifah (رَضِيَ اللَّهُ عَنْهُ): That he saw a man with a piece of twine on his hand (as protection or cure from fever) so he cut the twine and read the verse: «Most of them do not believe in Allāh except that they still practice Shirk (polytheism).» [12: 106] [1]

1 — Tafsīr al-Qurān al-'Aḍhīm of Ibn Abī Hātim : (7/2208)

ISSUES OF THIS CHAPTER:

1. The strict prohibition of wearing rings, twines, and the like.

2. If the Companion had died wearing such a thing, he would not have succeeded (in the Hereafter). This is a confirmation to the statement of the Companions that minor Shirk is greater (worse) than major sins.

3. Ignorance was no excuse.

4. Wearing any such things will not benefit anyone in this life. Indeed, it is harmful as was stated by the Prophet ( ) "It will do nothing except increase (the individual in) weakness."

5. The intense disapproval and censure of whoever does such a deed.

6. The affirmation that whoever attaches something to himself will have that thing put in charge of him.

7. The declaration that whoever wears an amulet has committed Shirk.

8. Hoping to get cured of a fever by using a talisman is Shirk.

9. Hudhaifah's (رَضِيَ ٱللَّهُ عَنْهُ) reciting of the verse in the Qur'ān is a clear-cut proof that Companions used to recite the verses dealing with the major Shirk to condemn minor Shirk. As Ibn 'Abbās (رَضِيَ ٱللَّهُ عَنْهُمَا) did by reciting the verse from Sūrah Al-Baqarah. (2: 165).

10. Seeking relief against the evil eye by using amulets is Shirk.

11. The curse on those who use amulets in that their wishes will not be granted by Allāh and those who use shells will not rest nor achieve peace. Allāh has left them.

CHAPTER EXERCISES

1. Explain the verse: "Most of them do not believe in Allāh except that they still practice Shirk (polytheism)." [12: 106]

2. Give one example where forbidding evil occurs in this chapter.

3. How does wearing objects to ward off evil add to one's weakness?

4. What is the definition of minor shirk?

5. Give two differences between major shirk and minor shirk?

CHAPTER EXERCISES

CHAPTER EXERCISES

CHAPTER 7:

What Has Come Regarding Ruqā, Talismans and Amulets

فِي الصَّحِيحِ عَنْ أَبِي بَشِيرٍ الأَنْصَارِيِّ؛ أَنَّهُ كَانَ مَعَ النَّبِيِّ صَلَّى ٱللَّهُ عَلَيْهِ وَسَلَّمَ في بعض أسفاره، فَأَرْسَلَ رَسُولًا: «أَنْ لَا يَبْقَيَنَّ فِي رَقَبَةِ بَعِيرٍ قِلَادَةٌ مِنْ وَتَرٍ - أَوْ: قِلَادَةٌ - إِلَّا قُطِعَتْ».

In an authentic narration, Abū Bashir Al-Ansari (رَضِيَ ٱللَّهُ عَنْهُ) narrated that he accompanied Allāh's Messenger (صَلَّى ٱللَّهُ عَلَيْهِ وَسَلَّمَ) on one of his journeys. He (صَلَّى ٱللَّهُ عَلَيْهِ وَسَلَّمَ) sent a messenger ordering him: "There must not remain any necklace of a bowstring or any other kind of necklace around the necks of camels except it is cut off."[1]

1 — Al-Bukhārī: (3005) and Muslim: (2115)

وَعَنِ ابْنِ مَسْعُودٍ رَضِيَٱللَّهُعَنْهُ قَالَ: سَمِعْتُ رَسُولَ اللهِ صَلَّىٱللَّهُعَلَيْهِوَسَلَّمَ يَقُولُ: « إِنَّ الرُّقَى وَالتَّمَائِمَ وَالتِّوَلَةَ شِرْكٌ». رَوَاهُ أَحْمَدُ وَأَبُو دَاوُدَ.

Ibn Mas'ūd (رَضِيَٱللَّهُعَنْهُ) narrated that he heard Allāh's Messenger (صَلَّىٱللَّهُعَلَيْهِوَسَلَّمَ) say: "Ar-Ruqā, At-Tamā'im, and At-Tiwalah are all acts of Shirk (polytheism)." It has been collected in the Musnad of Aḥmad and the Sunnan of Abī Dāwūd. [1]

1 — Al-Musnad: (6/110), Sunnan Abī Dāwūd: (4/137 no.5208), Ibn Mājah: (3530). Authenticated by al-Hākim and adh-Dhabī in Al- Mustadrak: 4/217,418) and Sh. al-Albānī in as-Silsilah aṣ-Ṣaḥīḥah: (331).

وَعَنْ عَبْدِ اللهِ بْنِ عُكَيْمٍ مَرْفُوعًا: «مَنْ تَعَلَّقَ شَيْئًا وُكِلَ إِلَيْهِ». رَوَاهُ أَحْمَدُ وَالتِّرْمِذِيُّ.

'Abdullāh b. Ukaīm narrated the following Marfū' Ḥadīth: "Whoever attaches anything (uses or wears a talisman) to himself, will have that thing put in charge of him." Collected in Aḥmad and at-Tirmidhī.[1]

---

1 — *Al-Musnad*: (31/77), *Sunan at-Tirmidhī*: (2072): This narration has a narrator called Muḥammad b. 'Abdur-Raḥmān b. Abī Laylah. Due to his overwhelming mistakes and poor memory (*at-Taqrīb*: 871 no 6121), this chain is weak. However, the previous narration from 'Uqabah (in *al-Musnad* of Imām Aḥmad: [28/623] and others), strengthen its meaning and authenticity making it ḥasan by external support from other narrations (ḥasan li ghairhi).

التَّمَائِمُ: شَيْءٌ يُعَلَّقُ عَلَى الأَوْلَادِ عَنِ الْعَيْنِ؛ لَكِنْ إِذَا كَانَ الْمُعَلَّقُ مِنَ الْقُرْآنِ فَرَخَّصَ فِيهِ بَعْضُ السَّلَفِ، وَبَعْضُهُمْ لَمْ يُرَخِّصْ فِيهِ، وَيَجْعَلُهُ مِنَ الْمَنْهِيِّ عَنْهُ؛ مِنْهُمُ ابْنُ مَسْعُودٍ رَضِيَ اللَّهُ عَنْهُ.

At-Tamā'im is the act of putting an amulet around the necks of children to save them from the effects of the evil eye! If the amulet contains the verses of the Qur'ān, then it is allowed by some of the salaf and disallowed by others. Ibn Mas'ūd (رَضِيَ اللَّهُ عَنْهُ) was from those who disapproved of it.

وَالرُّقَى هِيَ الَّتِي تُسَمَّى الْعَزَائِمَ، وَخَصَّ مِنْهُ الدَّلِيلُ مَا خَلَا مِنَ الشِّرْكِ، فَقَدْ رَخَّصَ فِيهِ رَسُولُ اللهِ مِنَ الْعَيْنِ وَالْحُمَةِ. وَالتِّوَلَةُ: شَيْءٌ يَصْنَعُونَهُ يَزْعُمُونَ أَنَّهُ يُحَبِّبُ الْمَرْأَةَ إِلَى زَوْجِهَا، وَالرَّجُلَ إِلَى امْرَأَتِهِ.

Ar-Ruqa or Al-Azā'im is the act of reciting incantations, charm, etc. Those are allowed in which there is no trace of Shirk (polytheism), Prophet Muḥammad (ﷺ) has permitted it in the case of one being bitten by poisonous insects or disturbed under the effect of an evil eye. At-Tiwalah (bewitchment) is something done by those who claim they can cause a woman to be more beloved to her husband or vice-versa.

وَرَوَى الْإِمَامُ أَحْمَدُ عَنْ رُوَيْفِعٍ قَالَ: قَالَ لِي رَسُولُ اللهِ ﷺ: «يَا رُوَيْفِعُ، لَعَلَّ الْحَيَاةَ سَتَطُولُ بِكَ، فَأَخْبِرِ النَّاسَ أَنَّ مَنْ عَقَدَ لِحْيَتَهُ، أَوْ تَقَلَّدَ وَتَرًا، أَوِ اسْتَنْجَى بِرَجِيعِ دَابَّةٍ أَوْ عَظْمٍ، فَإِنَّ مُحَمَّدًا بَرِيءٌ مِنْهُ»

Al-Imām Aḥmad reported that Ruwaifi'i (رضي الله عنه) who said that Allāh's Messenger (ﷺ) said to him: "O Ruwaifi'i, it may be that you will live a long life after me, so inform people that whoever ties a knot in his beard, places any string or cord around the neck (as a charm), or cleans himself (after toilet) with animal dung or bone, then Muḥammad (ﷺ) is free from him (has nothing to do with him)."

وَعَنْ سَعِيدِ بْنِ جُبَيْرٍ قَالَ: «مَنْ قَطَعَ تَمِيمَةً مِنْ إِنْسَانٍ كَانَ كَعَدْلِ رَقَبَةٍ». رَوَاهُ وَكِيعٌ. وَلَهُ عَنْ إِبْرَاهِيمَ: «كَانُوا يَكْرَهُونَ التَّمَائِمَ كُلَّهَا؛ مِنَ الْقُرْآنِ وَغَيْرِ الْقُرْآنِ».

Sa'īd bin Jubair said: "Whoever cuts an amulet or talisman from anyone, it would be equal to liberating a slave." It was Wakī', who recorded it and he reported from Ibrahim an-Nakha'ī that they used to dislike every type of amulets and talismans whether they contained the verses of Qur'ān or anything else.

ISSUES OF THIS CHAPTER:

1. Explanation of incantations (Ar-Ruqa) and amulets (At- Tama'im).
2. Explanation of bewitchment (At-Tiwalah).
3. That all three of the above-mentioned are acts of Shirk without exception.
4. Reciting an incantation (Ruqyah), using words of truth, for seeking protection from evil eye or scorpion bite is not like Shirk.
5. Scholars have different opinions regarding the use of amulets containing the verses of the Qur'ān.
6. Putting necklaces on animals to ward off the evil eye tantamounts to Shirk.
7. Anyone tying the bowstring (or committing such practices) has been warned of severe punishment.
8. The reward of a person who cuts off an amulet of someone.
9. The statement of Ibrāhīm an-Nakh'ī that early Muslims used to avoid amulets whether it contained Qur'anic verses or anything else is not contradictory as the reference here is to the companions of 'Abdullāh b. Mas'ūd (رَضِيَ اللَّهُ عَنْهُ).

CHAPTER EXERCISES

1. What is the relevance of this chapter to the previous one?

2. Why did the author mention in the previous (chapter 6) heading that wearing a ring, twine, and its likes for prevention or lifting of harm is an act of shirk, however, in this chapter he did not explicitly mention that ar-Ruqa and at-Tamā'im are acts of shirk?

3. Why did the Messenger (صَلَّالَلَّهُعَلَيْهِوَسَلَّمَ) say that the necklaces or bowstrings tied around the camels must be cut off?

4. What are the levels of commanding the good and forbidding the evil?

5. What prompted 'Abdullāh b. Mas'ūd (رَضِيَٱللَّهُعَنْهُ) to mention the ḥadīth: "Ar-Ruqa, At-Tamā'im, and At-Tiwalah are all acts of Shirk (polytheism)"?

CHAPTER EXERCISES

CHAPTER EXERCISES

CHAPTER EXERCISES

CHAPTER 8:

Whoever Seeks Blessings Through a Tree, a Stone, or the Like

وَقَوْلِ اللهِ تَعَالَى: «أَفَرَأَيْتُمُ اللَّاتَ وَالْعُزَّىٰ ۝ وَمَنَاةَ الثَّالِثَةَ الْأُخْرَىٰ» النجم الآيَاتِ.

Allāh the Most Exalted said: "Have you then considered Al-Lāt and Al-'Uzzā (the two idols of the pagan Arabs). And Manāt (another idol of the pagan Arabs), the other third one?" [53:19-20]

> عَنْ أَبِي وَاقِدٍ اللَّيْثِيِّ قَالَ: خَرَجْنَا مَعَ رَسُولِ اللهِ صَلَّىٱللَّهُعَلَيْهِوَسَلَّمَ إِلَى حُنَيْنٍ، وَنَحْنُ حُدَثَاءُ عَهْدٍ بِكُفْرٍ، وَلِلْمُشْرِكِينَ سِدْرَةٌ يَعْكُفُونَ عِنْدَهَا، وَيَنُوطُونَ بِهَا أَسْلِحَتَهُمْ، يُقَالُ لَهَا (ذَاتُ أَنْوَاطٍ)،
>
> Abū Wāqid Al-Laithī said: We went out with Allāh's Messenger (صَلَّىٱللَّهُعَلَيْهِوَسَلَّمَ) on the campaign of Hunain while we had just left the life of disbelief (Kufr) for Islām. The polytheist had a Sidra (lote-tree) that they would hang their arms on, called Dhat Anwat.

فَمَرَرْنَا بِسِدْرَةٍ، فَقُلْنَا: يَا رَسُولَ اللهِ؛ اجْعَلْ لَنَا ذَاتَ أَنْوَاطٍ كَمَا لَهُمْ ذَاتُ أَنْوَاطٍ، فَقَالَ رَسُولُ اللهِ ﷺ: «اللهُ أَكْبَرُ، إِنَّهَا السُّنَنُ، قُلْتُمْ وَالَّذِي نَفْسِي بِيَدِهِ كَمَا قَالَتْ بَنُو إِسْرَائِيلَ لِمُوسَى: ‹قَالُوا يَا مُوسَى اجْعَل لَّنَا إِلَٰهًا كَمَا لَهُمْ آلِهَةٌ قَالَ إِنَّكُمْ قَوْمٌ تَجْهَلُونَ› لَتَرْكَبُنَّ سَنَنَ مَنْ كَانَ قَبْلَكُمْ».
رَوَاهُ التِّرْمِذِيُّ وَصَحَّحَهُ.

When we passed a Sidra, we asked, "O Messenger of Allāh (ﷺ), won't you make for us another Dhat Anwat just like their Dhat Anwat?" Allāh's Messenger (ﷺ) said, "Allāhu Akbar (Allāh is the Greatest)! By the One (Allāh) Who holds my soul in His Hand, verily these are the ways of earlier nations, you have said exactly as Banī Isrāel said to Musa: 'Make for us a deity just as they have deities.' "He said: "'Verily you are an ignorant people.' (7:138) You will surely follow the ways of those who came before you." Reported by At-Tirmidhī who declared it as ṣaḥiḥ (authentic).[1]

1 — *Al-Musnad*: (36/225), at-Tirmidhī: (2180). Authenticated by at-Tirmidhī, and Sh. al-Albānī in *al-Mishkāh*: (5369)

ISSUES OF THIS CHAPTER:

1. Explanation of the verse (Sūrah An-Najm 53:19,20).
2. The nature of the matter requested by the companions (رَضِيَ ٱللَّهُ عَنْهُمْ) (regarding a tree similar to Dhat-Anwat).
3. The fact that the Companions (رَضِيَ ٱللَّهُ عَنْهُمْ) did not fall into it.
4. Their intention was to become closer to Allāh by their act as they thought He would like it.
5. If the Companions (رَضِيَ ٱللَّهُ عَنْهُمْ) were unaware of the nature of their intended action, it stands to reason that other than them (of much lesser status) are more likely to fall into ignorance.
6. For the Companions (رَضِيَ ٱللَّهُ عَنْهُمْ) is the reward of good deeds and the promise of forgiveness that is not for others.
7. The Prophet (صَلَّى ٱللَّهُ عَلَيْهِ وَسَلَّمَ) did not excuse them but denied by saying: "Allāhu Akbar, you will follow those who came before you" — thereby expressing the weightiness of the matter by these three things.
8. This is a major issue which is intended, that the Prophet (صَلَّى ٱللَّهُ عَلَيْهِ وَسَلَّمَ) informed them that their request was like that of Banī Isrāīl when they asked Mūsā (صَلَّى ٱللَّهُ عَلَيْهِ وَسَلَّمَ) "Make for us a diety."
9. The negation of this act is in essence the meaning of "There is no true deity worthy of worship except Allāh", which being subtle and hidden, was not perceived by them.
10. Swearing made by the Prophet (صَلَّى ٱللَّهُ عَلَيْهِ وَسَلَّمَ) upon the ruling and he did not ever swear except for a beneficial purpose.
11. Shirk is of two types, i.e. major and minor because the Companions (رَضِيَ ٱللَّهُ عَنْهُمْ) were not deemed apostates due to their request.
12. Their submission that "we had just left disbelief," tells us that other Companions (رَضِيَ ٱللَّهُ عَنْهُمْ) were not unaware of the matter.
13. The permissibility of saying Allāhu Akbar to express surprise. It contradicts the opinion of those who consider it undesirable (Makruh).
14. To put an end to all possible ways leading to Shirk (polytheism).

ISSUES OF THIS CHAPTER:

15. Prohibition of any resemblance with the people of ignorance (disbelievers).
16. A teacher can become unhappy with his students (for their betterment) while educating.
17. The general tendency of mankind has been expressed by the Prophet (صَلَّىٰ ٱللَّٰهُ عَلَيْهِ وَسَلَّمَ) by saying: "These are the ways".
18. It is one of the signs of the Prophethood that the events occurred accordingly as he informed.
19. In every place where Allāh has censured the Jews and Christians in the Qur'an, He has also warned us against those deeds.
20. The Companions (رَضِيَ ٱللَّٰهُ عَنْهُمْ) knew this principle that acts of worship are based on direct commandments. It, therefore, becomes a reminder concerning questions in the grave. The question "Who is your Lord"? is clear. The second question "Who is your Prophet?" depends on the information of the Prophet (صَلَّىٰ ٱللَّٰهُ عَلَيْهِ وَسَلَّمَ) regarding the unseen. But the third question "Which is your religion" is related to their (the Jews) request from Mūsā (صَلَّىٰ ٱللَّٰهُ عَلَيْهِ وَسَلَّمَ). "Make for us a diety".
21. That the ways of the People of the Book are condemned as those of the polytheists.
22. The one who has moved from falsehood (i.e. became Muslim) and get accustomed to certain beliefs or habits is not safe from having remnants of these habits as is evidenced in their (the Companions) words "and we had just left disbelief (Kufr)."

CHAPTER EXERCISES

1. What is the connection between this chapter and the two previous chapters?

2. What is the correct belief and understanding regarding one receiving blessings?

3. Where did the pagans derive the names; Al-Lāt , Al-'Uzzā, and Manāt from?

4. Why did the Messenger (صَلَّى ٱللَّهُ عَلَيْهِ وَسَلَّمَ) reprimand his companions (رَضِيَ ٱللَّهُ عَنْهُمْ) even though they recently embraced Islām?

5. What is the proof in this chapter for not following the ways of those before us from the Jews, Christians, and those who associated partners with Allāh?

CHAPTER EXERCISES

CHAPTER EXERCISES

CHAPTER 9:

Slaughtering for Other than Allāh

وَقَوْلِ اللهِ تَعَالَى: « قُلْ إِنَّ صَلَاتِي وَنُسُكِي وَمَحْيَايَ وَمَمَاتِي لِلَّهِ رَبِّ الْعَالَمِينَ ۝ لَا شَرِيكَ لَهُ» الأنعام. الآية

Allāh the Exalted said: "Say: Verily my prayer, my sacrifice, my living, and my dying are for Allāh, the Lord of all worlds. He has no partner. And of this, I have been commanded, and I am the first of the Muslims." [6:162,163]

وَقَوْلِهُ: « فَصَلِّ لِرَبِّكَ وَانْحَرْ « الكوثر: ٢

Allāh the Exalted also said: "Therefore turn in prayer to your Lord and sacrifice (to Him only)." [108:2]

عَنْ عَلِيِّ بْنِ أَبِي طَالِبٍ قَالَ: حَدَّثَنِي رَسُولُ اللهِ بِأَرْبَعِ كَلِمَاتٍ: «لَعَنَ اللهُ مَنْ ذَبَحَ لِغَيْرِ اللهِ، لَعَنَ اللهُ مَنْ لَعَنَ وَالِدَيْهِ،

Ali b. Abi Ṭālib (رَضِيَ اللَّهُ عَنْهُ) said: "Allāh's Messenger (صَلَّى اللَّهُ عَلَيْهِ وَسَلَّمَ) informed me about four statements: (1) Allāh's curse is upon the one who slaughters (devoting his sacrifice) to anything other than Allāh; (2) Allāh's curse is upon the one who curses his parents;

> لَعَنَ اللهُ مَنْ آوَى مُحْدِثًا، لَعَنَ اللهُ مَنْ غَيَّرَ مَنَارَ الأَرْضِ». رَوَاهُ مُسْلِمٌ.
>
> (3) Allāh's curse is upon the one who shelters a heretic (who has brought a Bid'ah in religion); (4) Allāh's curse is upon the one who alters the landmarks (who changes boundary lines)." Reported by Muslim.[1]

1 — Muslim: (1978)

وَعَنْ طَارِقِ بْنِ شِهَابٍ؛ أَنَّ رَسُولَ اللهِ قَالَ: «دَخَلَ الْجَنَّةَ رَجُلٌ فِي ذُبَابٍ، وَدَخَلَ النَّارَ رَجُلٌ فِي ذُبَابٍ»، قَالُوا: وَكَيْفَ ذَلِكَ يَا رَسُولَ اللهِ؟ قَالَ: «مَرَّ رَجُلَانِ عَلَى قَوْمٍ لَهُمْ صَنَمٌ، لَا يَجُوزُهُ أَحَدٌ حَتَّى يُقَرِّبَ لَهُ شَيْئًا، فَقَالُوا لِأَحَدِهِمَا: قَرِّبْ، قَالَ: لَيْسَ عِنْدِي شَيْءٌ أُقَرِّبُ

Ṭāriq b. Shihāb narrated that Allāh's Messenger (ﷺ) said: "A man entered Paradise because of a fly, and a man entered Hellfire because of a fly." They (the Companions) asked, "How was that possible O Messenger of Allāh (ﷺ)?" He said, "Two men passed by some people who had an idol by which they would not allow anyone to pass without making a sacrifice to it. They ordered one man to make a sacrifice. He said, 'I have nothing to present as an offering.'

قَالُوا لَهُ: قَرِّبْ وَلَوْ ذُبَابًا، فَقَرَّبَ ذُبَابًا؛ فَخَلَّوْا سَبِيلَهُ، فَدَخَلَ النَّارَ، وَقَالُوا لِلآخَرِ: قَرِّبْ، فَقَالَ: مَا كُنْتُ لِأُقَرِّبَ لِأَحَدٍ شَيْئًا دُونَ اللهِ عَزَّ وَجَلَّ، فَضَرَبُوا عُنُقَهُ، فَدَخَلَ الْجَنَّةَ». رَوَاهُ أَحْمَدُ.

The people told him, 'Sacrifice something, even if it be a fly.' So, he presented a fly (to their idol). They opened the way for him, and thus he entered the Hell-fire. They said to the other man, 'Sacrifice something.' He said, 'I will never sac-rifice anything to any other than Allāh, Most Majestic and Glorious.' They struck his throat and killed him; and he, therefore, entered Paradise." Collected by Aḥmad.[1]

1 — There is no evidence in the books of ḥadīth that this is from the statements of the Messenger of Allāh (صَلَّىٰ ٱللَّٰهُ عَلَيْهِ وَسَلَّمَ). In fact, it is authentically ascribed to Salmān al-Fārisī (رَضِيَ ٱللَّٰهُ عَنْهُ); Muṣanaf ibn Abī Shaybah: (17/537, no. 33709). The reference to Aḥmad here is to his *az-Zuhud*: (15-16). This narration is a statement of Salmān (رَضِيَ ٱللَّٰهُ عَنْهُ) (mawqūf). (See *as-Silsilah aḍ-Ḍa'īfah*: 12/723)

ISSUES OF THIS CHAPTER:

1. Explanation of the verse:

   "Verily my prayer, my sacrifice..."(6:162)

2. Explanation of the verse:

   "Therefore turn in prayer to your Lord and sacrifice to Him only." (108:2)

3. The beginning of the principle of cursing those who sacrifice to other than Allāh.
4. Curse is upon those who curse their parents (by cursing other parents and, in turn, the latter curses his parents).
5. Cursed is the person who shelters the heretic (Muhdith) in religion that is, he innovates something that is necessarily only Allāh's right to do and he seeks shelter with someone who assists him in it.
6. Curse upon him who unjustly alters the landmark, i.e. the boundaries that differentiate one person's land from his neighbor's, and changes those borders to encroach upon that land or obstruct it.
7. The difference between a specific curse and a curse upon the disobedient ones and rebels in general.
8. The tremendous story of the fly.
9. The person who presented a fly to the idol went to Hell though not intending to do such an act (beforehand). Indeed, he did it to save himself from the threat of idolaters.
10. Knowing the extent of how hated Shirk is to the hearts of the believers and seeing how the man was patient in facing execution and he did not give in to their demand even though they only demanded an external act from him.

11. The man who went to Hellfire was a Muslim. If he would have been a disbeliever (Kafir), the Prophet ( )would not have said: "He went to Hell merely for a fly."
12. This is a confirmation of the Ḥadīth "Paradise is closer to you than the laces of your shoes and the Hell-fire is likewise".
13. Recognition that the action of the heart is the main objective, even among the idol worshippers.

CHAPTER EXERCISES

1. What are the four affairs mentioned in this chapter that cause an individual to receive the curse of Allāh?

2. What is the ruling on the one that slaughters for other than Allāh?

3. What is the ruling on slaughtering an animal to feed your guest?

4. What is the difference between slaughtering a sheep to fulfill your duty as a host and slaughtering a sheep at a grave to get closer to its inhabitant?

5. Which verse mentioned in this chapter is proof of the obligation of sincerity at all times?

CHAPTER EXERCISES

CHAPTER EXERCISES

CHAPTER EXERCISES

CHAPTER EXERCISES

CHAPTER 10:

No Sacrifice for Allah Should be Done in a Place Where Sacrifice for Others is Made

> وَقَوْلِ اللهِ تَعَالَى: « لَا تَقُمْ فِيهِ أَبَدًا » التوبة: ١٠٨
>
> "Never stand (go) in there." [9:108]

عَنْ ثَابِتِ بْنِ الضَّحَّاكِ رَضِيَ اللَّهُ عَنْهُ قَالَ: نَذَرَ رَجُلٌ أَنْ يَنْحَرَ إِبِلًا بِبُوَانَةَ، فَسَأَلَ النَّبِيَّ صَلَّى اللَّهُ عَلَيْهِ وَسَلَّمَ، فَقَالَ: «هَلْ كَانَ فِيهَا وَثَنٌ مِنْ أَوْثَانِ الْجَاهِلِيَّةِ يُعْبَدُ؟»، قَالُوا: لَا، قَالَ: «فَهَلْ كَانَ فِيهَا عِيدٌ مِنْ أَعْيَادِهِمْ؟»، قَالُوا: لَا، فَقَالَ رَسُولُ اللهِ صَلَّى اللَّهُ عَلَيْهِ وَسَلَّمَ: «أَوْفِ بِنَذْرِكَ، فَإِنَّهُ لَا وَفَاءَ لِنَذْرٍ فِي مَعْصِيَةِ اللهِ، وَلَا فِيمَا لَا يَمْلِكُ ابْنُ آدَمَ». رَوَاهُ أَبُو دَاوُدَ، وَإِسْنَادُهُ عَلَى شَرْطِهِمَا.

Thābit b. Daḥḥāk (رَضِيَ اللَّهُ عَنْهُ) said: A man made a vow to sacrifice a camel at a place called Buwānah, so he asked the Prophet (صَلَّى اللَّهُ عَلَيْهِ وَسَلَّمَ) about its permissibility. He (صَلَّى اللَّهُ عَلَيْهِ وَسَلَّمَ) asked, "Does the place have an idol which is worshipped, from the idols of Jāhiliyah?" They answered, "No". The Prophet (صَلَّى اللَّهُ عَلَيْهِ وَسَلَّمَ) asked again, "Did the disbelievers hold any of their recurring festivities ('Īd) there?" They answered, "No." Allāh's Messenger (صَلَّى اللَّهُ عَلَيْهِ وَسَلَّمَ) then said, "Fulfill your vow. Verily there is no fulfilling of a vow made in disobedience to Allāh, nor one that is beyond a person's capacity." [Reported by Abū Dāwūd with a chain fitting the conditions of Al-Bukhārī and Muslim].[1]

1 — *Sunan* of Abī Dāwūd (3313). Shaykh al-Islām ibn Taymiyyah said: The origin of this narration is in al-Bukhārī and Muslim except that the chain of this ḥadīth — which is in line with the conditions of al-Bukhārī and Muslim — is specifically found in the *Sunan* of Abī Dāwūd. The chain has trustworthy, well known narrators and is connected with clear modes of transmission. (*al-Iqtiḍā*: 1/437),

ISSUES OF THIS CHAPTER:

1. The explanation of the verse: “Never you stand therein.”

2. That disobedience of Allāh leaves impressions on the earth as does obedience.

3. A problematic issue should be answered by a clear issue to eliminate any lack of clarity.

4. One who gives a religious verdict (Mufti) may ask for details if needed.

5. Vows can be specified for a particular place so long as that place is free from anything that would prohibit doing so.

6. It is prohibited to fulfill the vows in a place if there are idols of the times of ignorance even if the idolatry had ended.

7. It is prohibited to fulfill the vows in a place where disbelievers had celebrated any of their recurring festivities even it was stopped awhile ago.

8. A vow cannot be fulfilled what was made for any such place because it is considered a vow of disobedience (to Allāh).

9. A warning against resembling the polytheists in their celebrations even if it is unintended (i.e. the Muslim’s intention would not be the same as that of the polytheists).

10. There is no valid vow in the disobedience to Allāh.

11. No vow is valid for that which the children of Ādam does not possess.

CHAPTER EXERCISES

1. What is the difference between this chapter and the previous one?
2. Which masjid was intended in the verse “Never stand you therein” [9:108]?
3. What is the meaning of Jāhiliyah in the ḥadīth of Thābit (رَضِيَ ٱللَّهُ عَنْهُ)?
4. What is the meaning of ʿĪd (recurring festivities)?
5. How is the preservation of at-Tawḥīd emphasized in this chapter?

CHAPTER EXERCISES

CHAPTER 11:

To Vow to Other Than Allāh is an Act of Shirk

وَقَوْلِ اللهِ تَعَالَى: « يُوفُونَ بِالنَّذْرِ » الإنسان: ٧

وَقَوْلُهُ: «وَمَا أَنفَقْتُم مِّن نَّفَقَةٍ أَوْ نَذَرْتُم مِّن نَّذْرٍ فَإِنَّ اللَّهَ يَعْلَمُهُ البقرة» ٢٧٠

He, Most Exalted said: "They (are those who) fulfill (their) vows..." [76:7]

And He also said: "And whatever you spend (in Sadaqah charity etc.) or whatever vow you make, verily Allāh knows it all." [2:270]

وَفِي الصَّحِيحِ عَنْ عَائِشَةَ رَضِيَ اللَّهُ عَنْهَا ؛ أَنَّ رَسُولَ اللهِ صَلَّى اللَّهُ عَلَيْهِ وَسَلَّمَ قَالَ: «مَنْ نَذَرَ أَنْ يُطِيعَ اللهَ فَلْيُطِعْهُ، وَمَنْ نَذَرَ أَنْ يَعْصِيَ اللهَ فَلَا يَعْصِهِ».

In Al-Bukhārī 'Aishah (رَضِيَ اللَّهُ عَنْهَا) narrated that Allāh's Messenger (صَلَّى اللَّهُ عَلَيْهِ وَسَلَّمَ) said: "Whoever vows that he will be obedient to Allāh, he should be obedient to Him; and whoever made a vow that he will disobey Allāh, he should not disobey Him."[1]

1 — Al-Bukhārī: (6697)

ISSUES OF THIS CHAPTER:

1. The fulfillment of the vow is obligatory.
2. Since it is approved that making a vow is an act of worship to Allāh, then directing a vow to other than Allāh is an act of Shirk.
3. Any vow based on disobedience (to Allāh the Almighty) is impermissible to be carried out.

CHAPTER EXERCISES

1. What is the definition of a "vow"?
2. Give two examples of a vow of obedience.
3. Why is making a vow prohibited?
4. What is the proof from this chapter that making a vow is a type of worship?
5. What is the ruling on vowing to disobey Allāh? What is the proof for your answer?

CHAPTER EXERCISES

CHAPTER EXERCISES

CHAPTER 12:

From Shirk is to Seek Refuge in Other Than Allah

وَقَوْلِ اللهِ تَعَالَى: «وَأَنَّهُ كَانَ رِجَالٌ مِّنَ الْإِنسِ يَعُوذُونَ بِرِجَالٍ مِّنَ الْجِنِّ فَزَادُوهُمْ رَهَقًا» الجن: ٦

Allāh the Most Exalted said: "And verily, there were men among mankind who took shelter with the male jinns, but they (jinns) increased them (mankind) in sin and disbelief." [72:6]

وَعَنْ خَوْلَةَ بِنْتِ حَكِيمٍ رَضِيَ اللَّهُ عَنْهَا قَالَتْ: سَمِعْتُ رَسُولَ اللهِ صَلَّى اللَّهُ عَلَيْهِ وَسَلَّمَ يَقُولُ: «مَنْ نَزَلَ مَنْزِلًا فَقَالَ: أَعُوذُ بِكَلِمَاتِ اللهِ التَّامَّاتِ مِنْ شَرِّ مَا خَلَقَ، لَمْ يَضُرَّهُ شَيْءٌ حَتَّى يَرْحَلَ مِنْ مَنْزِلِهِ ذَلِكَ». رَوَاهُ مُسْلِمٌ.

Khawlah bint Hakīm (رَضِيَ اللَّهُ عَنْهَا) said, I heard Allāh's Messenger (صَلَّى اللَّهُ عَلَيْهِ وَسَلَّمَ) say: "Whoever goes into a dwelling and says (while entering it): 'I seek refuge in Allāh's perfect words from the evil which He created', no harm shall befall him until he departs from that place." Collected by Muslim.[1]

1 — Muslim: (2708)

ISSUES OF THIS CHAPTER:

1. Explanation of the verse from Surah Al-Jinn (72:6).

2. Seeking refuge in others than Allāh is a part of Shirk (polytheism).

3. Using this Ḥadīth as a proof: For, the scholars use it to prove that the Words of Allāh are not creatures. They say this because to seek refuge in creatures is Shirk.

4. The superiority of this invocation despite its being short.

5. Even though one can achieve some worldly benefit from a thing, as in prevention from harm or evil, or gaining some advantage or good, it does not mean that it is not Shirk.

CHAPTER EXERCISES

1. What are the ramifications of seeking refuge in the creation for that which is beyond their ability?

2. Give one proof from this chapter that the speech of Allāh, the Qur'ān is not created.

3. When is it permissible to seek aid from the creation?

4. Mention one proof that seeking refuge in Allāh is worship.

5. Give two virtues of the supplication mentioned in this chapter.

CHAPTER EXERCISES

CHAPTER EXERCISES

CHAPTER 13:

From Shirk is to Seek Deliverance from Other than Allah or Invoke Other than Him

وَقَوْلِ اللهِ تَعَالَى: «وَلَا تَدْعُ مِن دُونِ اللَّهِ مَا لَا يَنفَعُكَ وَلَا يَضُرُّكَ ۖ فَإِن فَعَلْتَ فَإِنَّكَ إِذًا مِّنَ الظَّالِمِينَ ۝ وَإِن يَمْسَسْكَ اللَّهُ بِضُرٍّ فَلَا كَاشِفَ لَهُ إِلَّا هُوَ» يونس: ١٠٦ - ١٠٧الآية

He the Most Exalted said: "And invoke not besides Allāh that which will neither profit you nor harm you, but if you did so, you shall certainly be one of the polytheists and wrongdoers. And if Allāh touches you with hurt, none can remove it but He." [10:106, 107]

وَقَوْلِهُ: « فَابْتَغُوا عِندَ اللَّهِ الرِّزْقَ وَاعْبُدُوهُ » الآيَةَ العنكبوت: ١٧

And He said: "So seek your provisions from Allāh (Alone) and worship Him (Alone)." [29:17]

وَقَوْلِهُ: «وَمَنْ أَضَلُّ مِمَّن يَدْعُو مِن دُونِ اللَّهِ مَن لَّا يَسْتَجِيبُ لَهُ إِلَىٰ يَوْمِ الْقِيَامَةِ »... الآيَتَيْنِ. الأحقاف: ٦,٥

وَقَوْلِهُ: « أَمَّن يُجِيبُ الْمُضْطَرَّ إِذَا دَعَاهُ وَيَكْشِفُ السُّوءَ » النمل: ٦٢

And He said: "And who is more astray than he who invokes besides Allāh those who will not respond to him until the Day of Resurrection..." [46: 5,6]. (With both verses)

And He said: "Is not He (better than your gods) Who responds to the distressed one, when he calls Him, and Who removes evil." [27:62]

وَرَوَى الطَّبَرَانِيُّ بِإِسْنَادِهِ؛ أَنَّهُ كَانَ فِي زَمَنِ النَّبِيِّ صَلَّى ٱللَّهُ عَلَيْهِ وَسَلَّمَ مُنَافِقٌ يُؤْذِي الْمُؤْمِنِينَ، فَقَالَ بَعْضُهُمْ: قُومُوا بِنَا نَسْتَغِيثُ بِرَسُولِ اللهِ صَلَّى ٱللَّهُ عَلَيْهِ وَسَلَّمَ مِنْ هَذَا الْمُنَافِقِ، فَقَالَ النَّبِيُّ صَلَّى ٱللَّهُ عَلَيْهِ وَسَلَّمَ: «إِنَّهُ لَا يُسْتَغَاثُ بِي، وَإِنَّمَا يُسْتَغَاثُ بِاللهِ عَزَّ وَجَلَّ».

At-Ṭabarānī narrated with his Isnad (chain of narrators): In the time of the Prophet (صَلَّى ٱللَّهُ عَلَيْهِ وَسَلَّمَ) there was a hypocrite who used to harm the believers, some of them (the believers) said, "Come with us so we can seek deliverance from Allāh's Messenger (صَلَّى ٱللَّهُ عَلَيْهِ وَسَلَّمَ) against this hypocrite." The Prophet (صَلَّى ٱللَّهُ عَلَيْهِ وَسَلَّمَ) replied, "Verily, no one should seek deliverance from me. Indeed, it is from Allāh (عَزَّ وَجَلَّ) deliverance is sought."[1]

1 — *al-Musnad*: (222706). *Majma' Al-Fawāid*: (10/159) Where al-Haythamī said: " All the narrators or from the men of al-Bukhārī and Muslim except for ibn Lahī'ā, therefore this ḥadīth is sound (ḥasan)."

ISSUES OF THIS CHAPTER:

1. To attach supplication or invocation (Du'a) with seeking assistance (Istighatha) using a conjunction is an example of attaching a general matter to a specific one.

2. Explanation of the verse:

> "And invoke not besides Allāh any that will neither profit you nor hurt you..." (10: 106).

3. This is the greater Shirk.

4. The most pious person, if he calls for help from other than Allāh, even for the gratification of someone else, he will become one of the Zalimun (wrong-doers, polytheists).

5. Explanation of the verse following (10: 107).

6. Calling others for help besides Allāh is of no benefit in this world and besides that, it is disbelief (Kufr).

7. Explanation of verse 29: 17.

8. Requesting sustenance and provisions should be from none other than Allāh. Just as Paradise can be requested from none other than Him.

9. Explanation of the fourth Verse 46:5.

10. There is none more misguided than the one who calls on others besides Allāh.

11. To whom the call is made to (besides Allāh) is unaware of the supplications of the caller; he knows nothing about it.

12. That call will be the cause of anger and enmity between the caller and the one called.

13. The call is named as the worship of the one being called upon.

14. The one called upon will deny and reject this act of worship towards him.

15. This is why such an individual (who falls into this act of shirk) is the most astray of the people.

16. Explanation of the fifth Verse 27: 62.

ISSUES OF THIS CHAPTER:

17. Astonishing is the admission of idolaters that none relieves the one in distress other than Allāh. That is why they call upon Him in times of extreme difficulty with the utmost religious sincerity.

18. The protection of the Chosen One (صَلَّى ٱللَّهُ عَلَيْهِ وَسَلَّمَ) means the protection of at-Tawḥīd and having good manners with Allāh.

CHAPTER EXERCISES

1. What is the ruling on seeking deliverance from other than Allāh?
2. Give two intellectual refutations against shirk in this chapter.
3. Give one proof from this chapter that Muḥammad (صَلَّى ٱللَّٰهُ عَلَيْهِ وَسَلَّمَ) is not a deity.
4. Give an example of the Messenger upholding and protecting the principles of at-Tawḥīd in this chapter.
5. Where in this chapter is the affirmation of Allāh's lordship being used to confirm that He deserves to be worshipped alone without any partners?

CHAPTER EXERCISES

CHAPTER EXERCISES

CHAPTER EXERCISES

CHAPTER 14:

"Do they ascribe partners with Allāh — those who created nothing but they themselves are created? No help can they give them..."

باب قَوْلِ اللهِ تَعَالَى: « أَيُشْرِكُونَ مَا لَا يَخْلُقُ شَيْئًا وَهُمْ يُخْلَقُونَ ۝ وَلَا يَسْتَطِيعُونَ لَهُمْ نَصْرًا » الآيَةَ. الأعراف: ١٩١ – ١٩٢

وَقَوْلِهِ: «وَالَّذِينَ تَدْعُونَ مِن دُونِهِ مَا يَمْلِكُونَ مِن قِطْمِيرٍ» الآيَةَ. فاطر: ١٣

Allāh The Most High said: "Do they attribute as partners to Allāh those who created nothing but they themselves are created? No help can they give them, nor can they help themselves." [7:191,192]

Allāh the Most Exalted said: "And those, whom you invoke or call upon besides Him, own not even a Qiṭmīr (the thin membrane over the date-stone)." [35:13]

وَفِي الصَّحِيحِ عَنْ أَنَسٍ قَالَ: شُجَّ النَّبِيُّ صَلَّى اللَّهُ عَلَيْهِ وَسَلَّمَ يَوْمَ أُحُدٍ، وَكُسِرَتْ رَبَاعِيَتُهُ، فَقَالَ: «كَيْفَ يُفْلِحُ قَوْمٌ شَجُّوا نَبِيَّهُمْ؟» فَنَزَلَتْ: ﴿ لَيْسَ لَكَ مِنَ الْأَمْرِ شَيْءٌ ﴾.

وَفِيهِ عَنِ ابْنِ عُمَرَ رَضِيَ اللَّهُ عَنْهُمَا: أَنَّهُ سَمِعَ رَسُولَ اللهِ صَلَّى اللَّهُ عَلَيْهِ وَسَلَّمَ يَقُولُ - إِذَا رَفَعَ رَأْسَهُ مِنَ الرُّكُوعِ فِي الرَّكْعَةِ الأَخِيرَةِ مِنَ الْفَجْرِ -: «اللَّهُمَّ الْعَنْ فُلَانًا وَفُلَانًا»، بَعْدَ مَا يَقُولُ: «سَمِعَ اللهُ لِمَنْ حَمِدَهُ، رَبَّنَا وَلَكَ الْحَمْدُ»؛ فَأَنْزَلَ اللهُ: ﴿ لَيْسَ لَكَ مِنَ الْأَمْرِ شَيْءٌ ﴾.

It is reported in the *Ṣaḥīḥ* from Anas (رَضِيَ اللَّهُ عَنْهُ) who narrated: The Prophet (صَلَّى اللَّهُ عَلَيْهِ وَسَلَّمَ) was hit on the day of Uḥud and his teeth were broken. He (صَلَّى اللَّهُ عَلَيْهِ وَسَلَّمَ) said, "How can people succeed who hit their Prophet?" The verse (3:128) was then revealed: "The decision is not for you." [1]

Ibn 'Umar (رَضِيَ اللَّهُ عَنْهُمَا) also reported that he heard Allāh's Messenger (صَلَّى اللَّهُ عَلَيْهِ وَسَلَّمَ) say when he raised his head from bowing in the last Rak'ah of the Fajr prayer: "O Allāh, curse so-and-so..." Afterwards he would say: "Allāh hears those that praise Him. O our Lord for you is all praise." Then Allāh revealed: "The decision is not for you." [2]

1 — Muslim: (1791) with a connected chain. In al-Bukhārī this narration is mentioned without a connecting chain (mu'allaqan) : (5/99 Dar Ṭūq an-Njāh)

2 — Al-Bukhārī: (4069)

وَفِي رِوَايَةٍ: يَدْعُو عَلَى صَفْوَانَ بْنِ أُمَيَّةَ، وَسُهَيْلِ بْنِ عَمْرٍو، وَالْحَارِثِ بْنِ هِشَامٍ، فَنَزَلَتْ: « لَيْسَ لَكَ مِنَ الْأَمْرِ شَيْءٌ »

In another narration: "He (ﷺ) invoked Allāh against Safwan b. Umaiyah and Suhail b. 'Amr and Al-Ḥārith b. Hishām", then the verse was revealed: 'Not for you (O Muḥammad, but for Allāh) is the decision.'"[1]

1 — Al-Bukhārī: (4070), *Al-Musnad*: (9/486) (with a connected chain) and at-Tirmidhī: (4004). This narration is authenticated by Sh. al-Albānī in *Ṣaḥīḥ Sunnan at-Tirmidhī* :(2402).

وَفِيهِ عَنْ أَبِي هُرَيْرَةَ رَضِيَ اللَّهُ عَنْهُ قَالَ: قَامَ رَسُولُ اللهِ صَلَّى اللَّهُ عَلَيْهِ وَسَلَّمَ حِينَ أُنْزِلَ عَلَيهِ: «وَأَنذِرْ عَشِيرَتَكَ الْأَقْرَبِينَ»، فَقَالَ: «يَا مَعْشَرَ قُرَيْشٍ - أَوْ كَلِمَةً نَحْوَهَا - اشْتَرُوا أَنفُسَكُمْ؛ لَا أُغْنِي عَنكُمْ مِنَ اللهِ شَيْئًا، يَا عَبَّاسُ بْنَ عَبْدِ الْمُطَّلِبِ لَا أُغْنِي عَنْكَ مِنَ اللهِ شَيْئًا، يَا صَفِيَّةُ - عَمَّةَ رَسُولِ اللهِ صَلَّى اللَّهُ عَلَيْهِ وَسَلَّمَ - لَا أُغْنِي عَنْكِ مِنَ اللهِ شَيْئًا، وَيَا فَاطِمَةُ بِنْتَ مُحَمَّدٍ، سَلِينِي مِنْ مَالِي مَا شِئْتِ، لَا أُغْنِي عَنْكِ مِنَ اللهِ شَيْئًا».

It is also reported in *Ṣaḥīḥ Al-Bukhārī* and Muslim from Abū Hurairah (رَضِيَ اللَّهُ عَنْهُ) who said: Allāh's Messenger (ﷺ) stood up when it was revealed to him: "And warn your tribe of near kindred." [26:214] He (ﷺ) said, "O people of Quraish" — or words similar to that effect — "Sell your own souls. I will not be of any help to you before Allāh; O 'Abbās b. 'Abdul-Muṭṭalib, I will not be of any help to you before Allāh; O Ṣafiyyah, aunt of Allāh's Messenger (ﷺ), I will not be of any help to you before Allāh; O Fatimah, daughter of Muḥammad, ask of my wealth what you wish, I will be of no avail to you before Allāh."[1]

1 — Al-Bukhārī:(2753), Muslim (206)

ISSUES OF THIS CHAPTER:

1. An explanation of the two verses (7:120 and 35:13,14).
2. The story of Uḥud.
3. Qunut (supplication) of Allāh's Messenger (ﷺ) in the prayer (against someones) and saying Amin of the Companions (رَضِيَ ٱللَّٰهُ عَنْهُمْ) behind him.
4. The ones who were supplicated against, were disbelievers (Kuffar).
5. They (Quraish) did things that most other of the disbelievers had not done such as causing injury to the head of their Prophet and being intent upon his murder. Also mutilation of those killed in battle though they were their cousins.
6. Allāh revealed to him about this:

> "Not for you (O Muḥammad, but for Allāh) is the decision."

7. His (Allāh's) Statement:

> "He turns in mercy to (pardons) them or punishes them" and He did turn toward them and they believed.

8. Al-Qunut (invoking Allāh against a people) in times of disaster.
9. Specifically naming the ones who are being invoked against in the prayers by their names and the names of their fathers.
10. Cursing someone in particular in the Qunut.
11. Circumstances of the Prophet (ﷺ) at the time of the revelation of : "And warn your tribe (O Muḥammad ﷺ) of near kindred." (26:214).
12. The seriousness of the Prophet (ﷺ) to the issue that insanity was attributed to him, and likewise is the case of a Muslim who does so now.

13. His (the Prophet's) statement to those close and far to him:

> "I will be of no avail to you before Allāh"

— to the extent that he said: "O Fatimah, daughter of Muḥammad, I will not be of any avail to you before Allāh."

ISSUES OF THIS CHAPTER:

If he made this clear while he was the leader of the Messengers — that he (صَلَّى ٱللَّهُ عَلَيْهِ وَسَلَّمَ) could not avail the best of women of this world, and a man believes that he (صَلَّى ٱللَّهُ عَلَيْهِ وَسَلَّمَ) does not speak but the truth, then he looks at what has occurred in the hearts of the people of position today, the issue of Tawḥīd would be clear, and so too the strangeness of the religion.

CHAPTER EXERCISES

1. Mention a place in this chapter where at-Tawhīd is emphasized.

2. What is the meaning of "curse" (اللعن)?

3. What were the names of the individuals the Messenger (صَلَّىٱللَّهُعَلَيْهِوَسَلَّمَ) invoked against?

4. Where in this chapter is proof that the Messenger of Allāh (صَلَّىٱللَّهُعَلَيْهِوَسَلَّمَ) does not know the unseen?

5. Where in this chapter is a refutation against nationalism and fanatic tribalism?

CHAPTER EXERCISES

CHAPTER EXERCISES

CHAPTER EXERCISES

CHAPTER 15:

"Until such time as fear is banished from their hearts..."

بَاب قَوْلِ اللهِ تَعَالَى: «حَتَّىٰ إِذَا فُزِّعَ عَن قُلُوبِهِمْ قَالُوا مَاذَا قَالَ رَبُّكُمْ ۖ قَالُوا الْحَقَّ ۖ وَهُوَ الْعَلِيُّ الْكَبِيرُ » سبأ: ٢٣

He, The Most High said: "Until such time as terror is removed from their hearts, they will say [to one another], 'What has your Lord said?' They will say, 'The truth.' And He is the Most High, the Great." [34:23]

فِي الصَّحِيحِ عَنْ أَبِي هُرَيْرَةَ ، عَنِ النَّبِيِّ قَالَ: «إِذَا قَضَى اللهُ الأَمْرَ فِي السَّمَاءِ ضَرَبَتِ الْمَلَائِكَةُ بِأَجْنِحَتِهَا خَضَعَانًا لِقَوْلِهِ، كَأَنَّهُ سلْسِلَةٌ عَلَى صَفْوَانٍ، يَنْفُذُهُمْ ذَلِكَ حَتَّى إذَا فُزِّعَ عَنْ قُلُوبِهِمْ؛ قَالُوا: مَاذَا قَالَ رَبُّكُمْ؟، قَالُوا: الْحَقَّ؛ وَهُوَ الْعَلِيُّ الْكَبِيرُ، فَيَسْمَعُهَا مُسْتَرِقُ السَّمْعِ، وَمُسْتَرِقُ السَّمْعِ هَكَذَا بَعْضُهُ فَوْقَ بَعْضٍ - وَصَفَهُ سُفْيَانُ بِكَفِّهِ، فَحَرَفَهَا وَبَدَّدَ بَيْنَ أَصَابِعِهِ

In the *Ṣaḥīḥ* from Abī Hurayrah (رَضِيَ اللَّهُ عَنْهُ) that the Prophet (صَلَّى اللَّهُ عَلَيْهِ وَسَلَّمَ) said: "When Allāh gives some order in the heaven, the angels flutter their wings indicating complete surrender to His Saying, which sounds like chains being dragged on a rock. And when the (state of) fear is banished from their hearts, they say, 'What is that your Lord has said?' They say: 'The truth. And He is the Most High, the Most Great.'" [34:23]

Then the stealthy listeners (devils) hear this order, and these stealthy listeners are like this, one over the other (Sufyan, a sub-narrator demonstrated that by holding his hand upright and separating the fingers)...

فَيَسْمَعُ الْكَلِمَةَ فَيُلْقِيْهَا إِلَى مَنْ تَحْتَهُ، ثُمَّ يُلْقِيْهَا الآخَرُ إِلَى مَنْ تَحْتَهُ، حَتَّى يُلْقِيَهَا عَلَى لِسَانِ السَّاحِرِ أَوِ الْكَاهِنِ، فَرُبَّمَا أَدْرَكَهُ الشِّهَابُ قَبْلَ أَنْ يُلْقِيَهَا، وَرُبَّمَا أَلْقَاهَا قَبْلَ أَنْ يُدْرِكَهُ، فَيَكْذِبُ مَعَهَا مِائَةَ كِذْبَةٍ، فَيُقَالُ: أَلَيْسَ قَدْ قَالَ لَنَا يَوْمَ كَذَا وَكَذَا: كَذَا وَكَذَا؟ فَيُصَدَّقُ بِتِلْكَ الْكَلِمَةِ الَّتِي سُمِعَتْ مِنَ السَّمَاءِ».

A stealthy listener hears a word which he will convey to those below him, and the second will convey it to the ones below him, till the last of them will convey it to the wizard or foreteller. Sometimes a flame (fire) may strike the devil before he can convey it, and sometimes he may convey it before the flame (fire) strikes him, whereupon the wizard adds to that word a hundred lies. The people will then say, 'Didn't he (i.e. magician) tell such-and-such a thing on such-and-such date?' So that magician is said to have told the truth because of the Statement which has been heard from the heavens." [1]

1 — Al-Bukhārī: (4701)

وَعَنِ النَّوَّاسِ بْنِ سَمْعَانَ رَضِيَ ٱللَّهُ عَنْهُ قَالَ: قَالَ رَسُولُ الله صَلَّى ٱللَّهُ عَلَيْهِ وَسَلَّمَ : «إِذَا أَرَادَ اللهُ تَعَالَى أَنْ يُوحِيَ بِالأَمْرِ، تَكَلَّمَ بِالْوَحْيِ أَخَذَتِ السَّمَاوَاتِ مِنْهُ رَجْفَةٌ - أَوْ قَالَ: رِعْدَةٌ - شَدِيدَةٌ، خَوْفًا مِنَ اللهِ عَزَّ وَجَلَّ، فَإِذَا سَمِعَ ذَلِكَ أَهْلُ السَّمَاوَاتِ صَعِقُوا وَخَرُّوا للهِ سُجَّدًا، فَيَكُونُ أَوَّلَ مَنْ يَرْفَعُ رَأْسَهُ جِبْرَائِيلُ، فَيُكَلِّمُهُ اللهُ مِنْ وَحْيِهِ بِمَا أَرَادَ، ثُمَّ يَمُرُّ جِبْرَائِيلُ عَلَى الْمَلَائِكَةِ، كُلَّمَا مَرَّ بِسَمَاءٍ سَأَلَهُ مَلَائِكَتُهَا: مَاذَا قَالَ رَبُّنَا يَا جِبْرَائِيلُ؟ فَيَقُولُ جِبْرَائِيلُ: قَالَ الْحَقَّ، وَهُوَ الْعَلِيُّ الْكَبِيرُ، فَيَقُولُونَ كُلُّهُمْ مِثْلَ مَا قَالَ جِبْرَائِيلُ، فَيَنْتَهِي جِبْرَائِيلُ بِالْوَحْيِ إِلَى حَيْثُ أَمَرَهُ اللهُ عَزَّ وَجَلَّ».

An-Nawwās b. Sam'ān (رَضِيَ ٱللَّهُ عَنْهُ) narrated that Allāh's Messenger (صَلَّى ٱللَّهُ عَلَيْهِ وَسَلَّمَ) said: "When Allāh wishes to reveal something to man, He speaks out the words to be revealed. The heavens then shake strongly in fear of Him. When the Words of Allāh fall upon the inhabitants of heaven, they are taken by shock and fall in prostration. The first of them to raise his head is the angel Jibrāīl whom Allāh speaks out of the revelation what He wishes. Then Jibrāīl passes by the other an-gels in different heavens, and is asked at each station, 'What did our Lord say, O Jibrāīl?' He answers: 'He said the Truth; He is the Most High, the Most Great,' and all repeat the same after him. Then Jibrāīl transmits the revelation to where Allāh the Most High commanded."[1]

1 — *Kitāb at-Tawhīd* of Ibn Khuzaymah: (1/236 no.206), *As-Sunnah* of ibn Abī 'Āṣīm: (1/360 no.527)

ISSUES OF THIS CHAPTER:

1. Explanation of verse 34:23.
2. In this verse is a proof for the falsehood of Shirk. Especially regarding what is attached to those righteous people (i.e. of the supplications of the ignorant toward them). It is said that this verse cuts the roots of the tree of Shirk in the heart.
3. Explanation of Allāh's Words:

   | "They say: 'The truth, and He is the Most High, the Most Great.'"

4. The reason for their question about that (verse).
5. That Jibrāīl answered their question after that by his words: "He said such and such."
6. The description of the fact that Jibrāīl was the first to raise his head.
7. Jibrāīl answers is to all angels of the heavens, as they all were asking him.
8. Unconsciousness occurs to all the dwellers of the heavens.
9. Trembling of the heavens due to the Words of Allāh.
10. That Jibrāīl is the one who conveys the revelation to wherever Allāh commands.
11. Eavesdropping of heavenly discussions by devils.
12. State of standing of Jinns on top of one another.
13. The Falling of shooting stars.
14. The shooting star sometimes hits the devil before he conveys the stolen message and sometimes he reaches the ear of his human recipient before he is struck.
15. Sometimes the soothsayer may relay the truth.
16. The soothsayer mixes the truth with a hundred lies.
17. His lies are not believed except for the word (of truth) which was heard from heaven.
18. The acceptance of falsehood by human nature. How they hang onto one truth and not consider the 100 lies.

ISSUES OF THIS CHAPTER:

19. How they pass the word to one another, memorize it and use it as evidence (for other lies).
20. Affirmation of the Divine Attributes of Allāh, in opposition to denials of the Ash'ariyah and Mu'attilah.
21. That the trembling and shaking of the heavens is due to the fear of Allāh the Almighty.
22. Angels fall in prostration for Allāh.

CHAPTER EXERCISES

1. Where in this chapter is proof that the angels are servants of Allāh, worshippers of Him?
2. Mention one virtue of Jibrīl mentioned in this chapter.
3. The speech of Allāh is affirmed in this chapter. Where?
4. Which other attributes of Allāh are affirmed in this chapter?
5. What is the relationship between soothsayers and the shayāṭīn (devils)?

CHAPTER EXERCISES

CHAPTER EXERCISES

CHAPTER 16:

Intercession

وَقَوْلِ اللهِ تَعَالَى: «وَأَنذِرْ بِهِ الَّذِينَ يَخَافُونَ أَن يُحْشَرُوا إِلَىٰ رَبِّهِمْ ۙ لَيْسَ لَهُم مِّن دُونِهِ وَلِيٌّ وَلَا شَفِيعٌ» الأنعام: ٥١

وَقَوْلُهُ: « قُل لِّلَّهِ الشَّفَاعَةُ جَمِيعًا » الزمر: ٤٤

Allāh the Almighty said: "And warn with it those who fear that they will be gathered before their Lord when there will neither be a protector nor an intercessor for them besides Him." [6:51]

He the Almighty said: "Say: To Allāh belongs all intercession." [39:44]

وَقَوْلُهُ: «مَن ذَا الَّذِي يَشْفَعُ عِندَهُ إِلَّا بِإِذْنِهِ» البقرة: ٢٥٥

وَقَوْلُهُ: «وَكَم مِّن مَّلَكٍ فِي السَّمَاوَاتِ لَا تُغْنِي شَفَاعَتُهُمْ شَيْئًا إِلَّا مِن بَعْدِ أَن يَأْذَنَ اللَّهُ لِمَن يَشَاءُ وَيَرْضَىٰ» النجم: ٢٦

He (Allāh) said: "Who is he that can intercede with Him except with His Permission..." [2:255]

He also said: "And there are many angels in the heavens whose intercession will not avail except after Allāh has permitted to whom He wills and is pleased with." [53:26]

وقولهِ: «قُلِ ادْعُوا الَّذِينَ زَعَمْتُم مِّن دُونِ اللَّهِ ۖ لَا يَمْلِكُونَ مِثْقَالَ ذَرَّةٍ فِي السَّمَاوَاتِ وَلَا فِي الْأَرْضِ» سبأ: ٢٢ الآيتين.

He said: "Say: Call upon those whom you assert besides Allāh, they do not even possess the weight of an atom (or a small ant), either in the heavens or on the earth..." [34:22,23] along with the verse after.[1]

---

1 — The entirety of the verses are:

> Say: Call upon those whom you assert besides Allāh, they do not even possess the weight of an atom (or a small ant), either in the heavens or on the earth, nor have they any share in either, nor there is for Him any supporter from among them.
>
> Intercession with Him profits not, except for him whom He permits. Until when fear is banished from their (angels') hearts, they (angels) say: "What is it that your Lord has said?" They say: "The truth. And He is the Most High, the Most Great."

قَالَ أَبُو الْعَبَّاسِ: «نَفَى اللهُ عَمَّا سِوَاهُ كُلَّ مَا يَتَعَلَّقُ بِهِ المشركين، فَنَفَى أَنْ يَكُونَ لِغَيْرِهِ مِلْكٌ، أَوْ قِسْطٌ مِنْهُ، أَوْ يَكُونَ عَوْنًا للهِ، وَلَمْ يَبْقَ إِلَّا الشَّفَاعَةُ، فَبَيَّنَ أَنَّهَا لَا تَنْفَعُ إِلَّا لِمَنْ أَذِنَ لَهُ الرَّبُّ، كَمَا قَالَ: ﴿ وَلَا يَشْفَعُونَ إِلَّا لِمَنِ ارْتَضَىٰ ﴾» الأنبياء: ٢٨.

Abul-'Abbās[1] said that Allāh has equally negated all that the Mushrikīn have clinged onto from their false dieties. He has negated that anyone has any dominion or any share of it besides Him, or that there is an assistant to Him, and that there is nothing to remain except intercession. He clarifies that intercessions will be of no benefit to anyone except for those who have been granted permission by the Lord as He stated: "They will not be able to intercede except for those whom He is pleased with." [21:28]

1 — Shaykh al-Islām Aḥmad b. 'Abdil- Ḥalīm al-Ḥarrānī — known as Ibn Taymiyyah (رَحِمَهُ ٱللَّهُ).

فَهَذِهِ الشَّفَاعَةُ الَّتِي يَظُنُّهَا الْمُشْرِكُونَ هِيَ مُنْتَفِيَةٌ يَوْمَ الْقِيَامَةِ، كَمَا نَفَاهَا الْقُرْآنُ، وَأَخْبَرَ النَّبِيُّ ﷺ أَنَّهُ يَأْتِي فَيَسْجُدُ لِرَبِّهِ وَيَحْمَدُهُ - لَا يَبْدَأُ بِالشَّفَاعَةِ أَوَّلًا - ثُمَّ يُقَالُ لَهُ: «ارْفَعْ رَأْسَكَ، وَقُلْ يُسْمَعْ، وَسَلْ تُعْطَ، وَاشْفَعْ تُشَفَّعْ». وَقَالَ لَهُ أَبُو هُرَيْرَةَ : مَنْ أَسْعَدُ النَّاسِ بِشَفَاعَتِكَ؟ قَالَ : «مَنْ قَالَ: لَا إِلَهَ إِلَّا اللهُ خَالِصًا مِنْ قَلْبِهِ»، فَتِلْكَ الشَّفَاعَةُ لِأَهْلِ الإِخْلَاصِ بِإِذْنِ اللهِ، وَلَا تَكُونُ لِمَنْ أَشْرَكَ بِاللهِ.

And for this reason, the intercession that the polytheists believe in is rejected on the Day of Resurrection, as it is rejected by the Qur'ān and as the Prophet (ﷺ) informed us that he will come and prostrate to his Lord and praise Him, and he will not begin with the intercession at first. It will be said afterwards: "Raise your head, speak and you will be heard, ask and you will be given, intercede and your intercession will be granted."[1]

Abū Hurayrah (رضي الله عنه) asked the Prophet (ﷺ): "Who will be the happiest of people with your intercession?" He (ﷺ) said, "Whoever said La ilāhā illa Allāh sincerely with pure intention from his heart."[2] So this intercession is for those people with sincerity, if Allāh wills, and it will not be for those who commit Shirk.

1 — Al-Bukhārī: (7510), Muslim: (193). Narrated by Anas b. Mālik (رضي الله عنه).

2 — Al-Bukhārī: (99), Narrated by Abī Hurairah (رضي الله عنه).

وَحَقِيقَتُهُ: أَنَّ اللهَ سُبْحَانَهُ هُوَ الَّذِي يَتَفَضَّلُ عَلَى أَهْلِ الإِخْلَاصِ، فَيَغْفِرُ لَهُمْ بِوَاسِطَةِ دُعَاءِ مَنْ أَذِنَ لَهُ أَنْ يَشْفَعَ لِيُكْرِمَهُ، وَيَنَالَ الْمَقَامَ الْمَحْمُودَ. فَالشَّفَاعَةُ الَّتِي نَفَاهَا الْقُرْآنُ مَا كَانَ فِيهَا شِرْكٌ، وَلِهَذَا أَثْبَتَ الشَّفَاعَةَ بِإِذْنِهِ فِي مَوَاضِعَ، وَقَدْ بَيَّنَ النَّبِيُّ صَلَّى اللهُ عَلَيْهِ وَسَلَّمَ أَنَّهَا لَا تَكُونُ إِلَّا لِأَهْلِ التَّوْحِيدِ وَالإِخْلَاصِ». انْتَهَى كَلَامُهُ.

The essence of the matter is that it is Allāh — the one above all imperfections — who favors the sincere worshippers and forgives them through the invocation of whoever He has permitted to intercede as an honor to him and for him to obtain the Highest Place (Al-Maqām-al-Maḥmūd).

Therefore, the intercession which is rejected and denied in the Qur'ān is that which involves Shirk, and this is why intercession is confirmed and affirmed by the permission of Allāh in many places. The Prophet (صَلَّى اللهُ عَلَيْهِ وَسَلَّمَ) made it clear that this intercession will not be for other than the people of at-Tawhīd (Islamic Monotheism) and ikhlās (sincerity). [End of quote]

ISSUES OF THIS CHAPTER:

1. Explanation of the verses mentioned.

2. Description of the rejected intercession.

3. Description of the affirmed intercession.

4. The "Greatest Intercession" being the "Highest Place" of the Prophet (صَلَّى ٱللَّهُ عَلَيْهِ وَسَلَّمَ).

5. A description of what the Prophet (صَلَّى ٱللَّهُ عَلَيْهِ وَسَلَّمَ) will do (on the Day of Judgement) and that he will not begin by making intercession, rather he will prostrate and when he is given permission he will intercede.

6. Who would be the happiest of people with the intercession of the Prophet (صَلَّى ٱللَّهُ عَلَيْهِ وَسَلَّمَ)?

7. Intercession will not be for those who commit Shirk.

8. Clarification of the real state of intercession.

CHAPTER EXERCISES

1. What are the conditions for a valid intercession?
2. Where in this chapter is proof that Allāh alone deserves to be worshipped with no partners?
3. Show one intellectual proof from the Qur'ān mentioned in this chapter that refutes those who call upon other than Allāh?
4. What kind of intercession is invalid and rejected?
5. Identify one major virtue of sincerity and at-Tawhīd taken from this chapter.

CHAPTER EXERCISES

CHAPTER EXERCISES

CHAPTER EXERCISES

CHAPTER 17:

"Verily, you do not guide whom you like..."

بَابُ قَوْلِ اللهِ تَعَالَى: « إِنَّكَ لَا تَهْدِي مَنْ أَحْبَبْتَ» القصص: ٥٦

فِي الصَّحِيحِ عَنِ ابْنِ الْمُسَيَّبِ، عَنْ أَبِيهِ قَالَ: لَمَّا حَضَرَتْ أَبَا طَالِبٍ الْوَفَاةُ، جَاءَهُ رَسُولُ اللهِ☒، وَعِنْدَهُ عَبْدُ اللهِ بْنُ أَبِي أُمَيَّةَ وَأَبُو جَهْلٍ، فَقَالَ لَهُ: «يَا عَمِّ، قُلْ: لَا إِلَهَ إِلَّا اللهُ، كَلِمَةً أُحَاجُّ لَكَ بِهَا عِنْدَ اللهِ»، فَقَالَا لَهُ: أَتَرْغَبُ عَنْ مِلَّةِ عَبْدِ الْمُطَّلِبِ؟

"Verily, you (O Muḥammad) do not guide whom you like." [28:56]

In the *Ṣaḥīḥ*, Ibn Al-Musayyab has reported from his father: "When death approached Abū Ṭālib, Allāh's Messenger (ﷺ) came to him and found `Abdullāh b. Abī Umaiyah and Abū Jahl with him. The Prophet (ﷺ) said, "O uncle, say: 'There is none that deserves to be worshiped except Allāh' — a word which will enable me to plead for you with Allāh." The two of them said, "Would you forsake the religion of 'Abdul-Muṭṭalib?!"

فَأَعَادَ عَلَيْهِ النَّبِيُّ ، فَأَعَادَا، فَكَانَ آخِرَ مَا قَالَ: هُوَ عَلَى مِلَّةِ عَبْدِ الْمُطَّلِبِ، وَأَبَى أَنْ يَقُولَ: لَا إِلَهَ إِلَّا اللهُ، فَقَالَ النَّبِيُّ : «لأَسْتَغْفِرَنَّ لَكَ، مَا لَمْ أُنْهَ عَنْكَ»، فَأَنْزَلَ اللهُ عَزَّ وَجَلَّ: ﴿مَا كَانَ لِلنَّبِيِّ وَالَّذِينَ آمَنُوا أَن يَسْتَغْفِرُوا لِلْمُشْرِكِينَ وَلَوْ كَانُوا أُولِي قُرْبَىٰ﴾. وَأَنْزَلَ اللهُ فِي أَبِي طَالِبٍ: ﴿إِنَّكَ لَا تَهْدِي مَنْ أَحْبَبْتَ وَلَٰكِنَّ اللَّهَ يَهْدِي مَن يَشَاءُ﴾.

The Prophet (ﷺ) repeated (the request) and the two of them also repeated (their question). The final word of Abū Ṭālib was that he was upon the religion of 'Abdul-Muṭṭalib and he refused to say: *Lā ilāhā illa-Allāh.* The Prophet (ﷺ) said: " I shall continue to pray for your forgiveness as long as I am not prohibited to do so." It was then that Allāh the Almighty revealed the verse: "It is not (befitting) for the Prophet and those who believe, to ask Allāh's forgiveness for the Mushrikīn even though they be of kin." [9:113]

Allāh also revealed concerning Abū Ṭālib: "Verily, you (O Muhammad) do not guide whom you like, but Allāh guides whom He wills." [28:56] [1]

1 — Al-Bukhārī: (1360) and Muslim: (24)

ISSUES OF THIS CHAPTER:

1. Explanation of the verse:

> "Verily, you (O Muḥammad) do not guide whom you like, but Allāh guides whom He wills. And He knows best those who are the guided ones." (28:56).

2. 2) Explanation of the verse:

> "It is not (proper) for the Prophet (صَلَّى ٱللَّهُ عَلَيْهِ وَسَلَّمَ) and those who believe to ask Allāh's Forgiveness for the Mushrikun (polytheists, idolaters, pagans, disbelievers in the Oneness of Allāh) even though they be of kin after it has become clear to them that they are the dwellers of the Fire (because they died in a state of disbelief)." [9: 113].

3. It is a major issue in the explanation of the statement of the Prophet (صَلَّى ٱللَّهُ عَلَيْهِ وَسَلَّمَ) "Say *Lā ilāha illā-Allāh*." Differing with those who claim to be possessing (religious) knowledge. (They claim it sufficient to be forgiven by merely uttering Kalimah).

4. Abū Jahl and those who were with him knew full well the intent of the Prophet (صَلَّى ٱللَّهُ عَلَيْهِ وَسَلَّمَ) when he said to the man (his uncle) "Say *Lā ilāha illā-Allāh*." May Allāh denounce the ones who were less knowledgeable than Abū Jahl regarding Islam.

5. The eagerness and intense desire of the Prophet (صَلَّى ٱللَّهُ عَلَيْهِ وَسَلَّمَ) to revert his uncle to Islam.

6. The denial of those who claim that 'Abdul-Muṭṭalib and his forefathers were Muslims.

7. Allāh did not forgive Abu Ṭālib despite the Prophet's initial asking forgiveness for him. On the contrary, he (صَلَّى ٱللَّهُ عَلَيْهِ وَسَلَّمَ) was forbidden to do so.

8. The harmful influence that evil companions can have on people.

9. The harm of overpraising ancestors and important personalities.

10. The arguments of falsifiers are the arguments of Jahiliyah (pre-Islamic period).

ISSUES OF THIS CHAPTER:

11. An attestation to the weight of the final deeds in one's life because had Abu Ṭālib confessed that there is no true deity (that deserves to be worshiped) except Allāh, it would have benefited him.

12. The consideration of the magnitude of this false argument in the hearts of the misguided, because in the story they did not argue except with it despite the intense effort of the Prophet (صَلَّى ٱللَّهُ عَلَيْهِ وَسَلَّمَ) and his repetition (of the Kalimah). Because of their tremendous pride (in ancestry) and its potency among them, they were content with it.

CHAPTER EXERCISES

1. What are the two different types of guidance? Which one is exclusively from Allāh (تَبَارَكَ وَتَعَالَىٰ)?

2. Where in this chapter is an example of the ill effects of bad companionship?

3. The Salaf detested shirk. Can you identify an example of this in this chapter?

4. Where is the connection between this chapter and at-Tawhīd?

5. Mention two additional benefits we can take from the story of the death of Abī Ṭālib?

CHAPTER EXERCISES

CHAPTER EXERCISES

CHAPTER EXERCISES

CHAPTER 18:

Exaggeration in the Righteous is the Root Cause for Mankind's Disbelief and Leaving the Religion

وَقَـوْلِ اللـهِ عَزَّوَجَلَّ : «يَـا أَهْـلَ الْكِتَـابِ لَا تَغْلُـوا فِـي دِينِكُـمْ وَلَا تَقُولُـوا عَلَـى اللَّـهِ إِلَّا الْحَـقَّ» النساء: ١٧١.

فِي الصَّحِيحِ عَنِ ابْنِ عَبَّاسٍ رَضِيَ اللَّهُ عَنْهُمَا فِي قَوْلِهِ تَعَالَى «وَقَالُوا لَا تَذَرُنَّ آلِهَتَكُمْ وَلَا تَذَرُنَّ وَدًّا وَلَا سُوَاعًا وَلَا يَغُوثَ وَيَعُوقَ وَنَسْرًا» نوح: ٢٣ ؛ قَالَ: «هَذِهِ أَسْمَاءُ رِجَالٍ صَالِحِينَ مِنْ قَوْمِ نُوحٍ، فَلَمَّا هَلَكُوا أَوْحَى الشَّيْطَانُ إِلَى قَوْمِهِمْ؛ أَنِ انْصِبُوا إِلَى مَجَالِسِهِمُ الَّتِي كَانُوا يَجْلِسُونَ فِيهَا أَنْصَابًا، وَسَمُّوهَا بِأَسْمَائِهِمْ، فَفَعَلُوا، وَلَمْ تُعْبَدْ، حَتَّى إِذَا هَلَكَ أُولَئِكَ وَنُسِيَ الْعِلْمُ عُبِدَتْ».

The Statement of Allāh the Almighty and Most Exalted: "O People of the Scripture (Jews and Christians)! Do not exceed the limits in your religion, nor say of Allāh anything but the truth..." [4:171]

In the *Ṣaḥiḥ*, Ibn 'Abbās (رَضِيَ اللَّهُ عَنْهُمَا) commented on the verse: "And they have said: You shall not leave your gods, you shall not leave Wadd nor Suwā' nor Yaghūth nor Ya'ūq nor Nasr." [71:23]

He said: "These are the names of some righteous people from Nuḥ's people. When they died, Shayṭān inspired them to set up statues in their honor, placed in their gatherings. They gave these statues the names of those righteous people. At this point, they did not worship them until they passed away and knowledge of their origins were forgotten, the statues were then worshipped."[1]

1 — Al-Bukhārī: (4920)

> وَقَالَ ابْنُ الْقَيِّمِ: «قَالَ غَيْرُ وَاحِدٍ مِنَ السَّلَفِ: لَمَّا مَاتُوا عَكَفُوا عَلَى قُبُورِهِمْ، ثُمَّ صَوَّرُوا تَمَاثِيلَهُمْ، ثُمَّ طَالَ عَلَيْهِمُ الأَمَدُ فَعَبَدُوهُمْ».
>
> Ibn Al-Qayyim said: "More than one of the Salaf have stated: After the death (of the righteous people), they confined at their graves and made statues and after a long period had passed, the people started worshipping them." [1]

1 — *Ighāthatu al-Lahfān*: (1/184)

وَعَنْ عُمَرَ؛ أَنَّ رَسُولَ اللهِ صَلَّى ٱللَّهُ عَلَيْهِ وَسَلَّمَ قَالَ: «لَا تُطْرُونِي كَمَا أَطْرَتِ النَّصَارَى ابْنَ مَرْيَمَ، إِنَّمَا أَنَا عَبْدٌ، فَقُولُوا: عَبْدُ اللهِ وَرَسُولُهُ». أَخْرَجَاهُ.] [قَالَ: قَالَ رَسُولُ اللهِ صَلَّى ٱللَّهُ عَلَيْهِ وَسَلَّمَ: «إِيَّاكُمْ وَالْغُلُوَّ، فَإِنَّمَا أَهْلَكَ مَنْ كَانَ قَبْلَكُمُ الْغُلُوُّ».

وَلِمُسْلِمٍ عَنِ ابْنِ مَسْعُودٍ رَضِيَ ٱللَّهُ عَنْهُ؛ أَنَّ رَسُولَ اللهِ صَلَّى ٱللَّهُ عَلَيْهِ وَسَلَّمَ قَالَ: «هَلَكَ الْمُتَنَطِّعُونَ»، قَالَهَا ثَلَاثًا.

'Umar (رَضِيَ ٱللَّهُ عَنْهُ) said that Allāh's Messenger (صَلَّى ٱللَّهُ عَلَيْهِ وَسَلَّمَ) said: "Do not exaggerate in praise of me as the Christians exaggerated in the praise of Jesus, son of Mary. I am only a slave, so call me Allāh's slave and His Messenger." (Al-Bukhārī and Muslim) [1]

Allāh's Messenger (صَلَّى ٱللَّهُ عَلَيْهِ وَسَلَّمَ) said: "Stay away from exaggeration. Those before you perished on account of their exaggeration."[2]

In (*Sahīh*) Muslim, 'Abdullāh b. Mas'ūd (رَضِيَ ٱللَّهُ عَنْهُ) reported that Allāh's Messenger (صَلَّى ٱللَّهُ عَلَيْهِ وَسَلَّمَ) said: "Those who are extreme are destroyed." He (صَلَّى ٱللَّهُ عَلَيْهِ وَسَلَّمَ) said it three times. [3]

---

1 — Al-Bukhārī: (3445). This narration has not been found in *Ṣaḥīḥ Muslim.*

2 — *Al-Musnad*: (3/350), An-Nasā'ī: (3057), Ibn Mājah: (3029). Authenticated by Ibn Taymiyyah: *al-Iqtiḍā* (1/293) , Sh. Sulaymān Āali as-Shaykh: *Taysīr al-'Azīz al-Ḥamīd*: (265) and Sh. al-Albānī : *aṣ-Ṣaḥīḥah*: (1283). This narration is reported by 'Abdullah b. 'Abbās (رَضِيَ ٱللَّهُ عَنْهُمَا).

3 — Muslim: (2670)

ISSUES OF THIS CHAPTER:

1. Whoever understood this chapter and the following two, will recognize the "strangeness" of Islam and see Allāh's wondrous power and wisdom to change hearts.

2. Recognition that the first Shirk commited on earth happened due to misconceptions regarding righteous people (and their piety).

3. Knowledge of the first thing that caused deviation from the religion of the Prophets and the reason for that, despite the knowledge that they were sent from Allāh.

4. The acceptance of innovations (by many)even though it is against legal laws and inborn nature.

5. The reason for all of that is the mixing of truth with falsehood: firstly, the exaggeration in the love of the righteous; and secondly, the action of people with religious knowledge intending to do good. However, the later generations thought that they intended something else.

6. Explanation of the verse in Surah Nuh (71:23).

7. Human nature (in general) towards the truth weakens in the heart while falsehood increases. (Except those guided and blessed by Allāh).

8. It confirms the sayings of our righteous predecessors that innovations (Bid'ah) is the main cause leading to Kufr (disbelief) [and that it (Bid'ah) is more beloved to Iblis than sinfulness because one may repent from sins but will not repent from Bid'ah].

9. Shayṭān (the devil) knows what the result of heresy is, even if commited with good intentions.

10. Knowledge of the general rule that excess and exaggeration (for the righteous) is prohibited, and knowledge of what it leads to.

11. The harm of seclusion at the grave even with the intention of performing a righteous deed.

12. The prohibition against statues and the wisdom behind destroying them.

13. The greatness of the matter within this story and how badly it is needed (i.e. the lesson within) in the face of the heedlessness and neglect of it.

ISSUES OF THIS CHAPTER:

14. It is amazing! And more amazing is that despite their (people of Bid'ah) reading this story in the books of Tafsir and Ḥadīth, along with their understanding of its meaning, and knowing about the obstruction that Allāh has put between them and their hearts, they believed that the deed of the people of Nuh (i.e. overpraising the dead and memorializing their graves with statues) is the best type of worship. They believed in what Allāh and His Messenger (صَلَّى ٱللَّهُ عَلَيْهِ وَسَلَّمَ) have forbidden which is the disbelief (Kufr) that permits the taking of life and wealth!

15. The declaration that they only wished the righteous ones to intercede for them.

16. Their assumption that those scholars who first shaped the statues had intended (exaggeration) by doing so.

17. The tremendous statement of Prophet Muḥammad (صَلَّى ٱللَّهُ عَلَيْهِ وَسَلَّمَ) "Do not exaggerate in praise of me just as the Christians had exaggerated in the praise of Jesus, son of Mary." May the peace and blessing of Allāh be upon him who has conveyed the clear message!

18. The admonition by the Prophet (صَلَّى ٱللَّهُ عَلَيْهِ وَسَلَّمَ) to us of the destruction of those going to extremes in the religion.

19. The clear statement that they (the statues) were not worshipped until true knowledge was forgotten. This explains the value of the presence of knowledge and the harm of losing it.

20. The reason for the loss of knowledge is the death of scholars.

CHAPTER EXERCISES

1. What were the names of the idols worshipped in the time of Nūḥ (صَلَّى ٱللَّهُ عَلَيْهِ وَسَلَّمَ)?
2. Where in this chapter can we find the proof for closing the gates that lead to evil from the offset?
3. What was the reason why the first act of shirk occurred?
4. How, in this chapter, can we say that bid'ah is a means to disbelief?
5. The ramifications of ignorance are shown in this Chapter? How?

CHAPTER EXERCISES

CHAPTER EXERCISES

CHAPTER 19:

Condemnation of the One Who Worships Allah at a Righteous Man's Grave. What if he actually Worships the Man!

فِي الصَّحِيحِ عَنْ عَائِشَةَ رَضِيَ اللَّهُ عَنْهَا؛ أَنَّ أُمَّ سَلَمَةَ رَضِيَ اللَّهُ عَنْهَا ذَكَرَتْ لِرَسُولِ اللهِ صَلَّى اللَّهُ عَلَيْهِ وَسَلَّمَ كَنِيسَةً رَأَتْهَا بِأَرْضِ الْحَبَشَةِ، وَمَا فِيهَا مِنَ الصُّوَرِ، فَقَالَ: «أُولَئِكَ إِذَا مَاتَ فِيهِمُ الرَّجُلُ الصَّالِحُ، أَوِ الْعَبْدُ الصَّالِحُ، بَنَوْا عَلَى قَبْرِهِ مَسْجِدًا، وَصَوَّرُوا فِيهِ تِلْكَ الصُّوَرَ، أُولَئِكَ شِرَارُ الْخَلْقِ عِنْدَ اللهِ». فَهَؤُلَاءِ جَمَعُوا بَيْنَ الْفِتْنَتَيْنِ: فِتْنَةِ الْقُبُورِ، وَفِتْنَةِ التَّمَاثِيلِ.

In the *Ṣaḥiḥ*, 'Āishah (رَضِيَ اللَّهُ عَنْهَا) reported: "Umm Salamah (رَضِيَ اللَّهُ عَنْهَا) mentioned to Allāh's Messenger (صَلَّى اللَّهُ عَلَيْهِ وَسَلَّمَ) that in Abyssinia she saw a church full of pictures and statues. He (صَلَّى اللَّهُ عَلَيْهِ وَسَلَّمَ) said: 'When a righteous man or pious worshipper among them dies they build a place of worship over his grave and set up all kinds of pictures and statues. They are the worst of all creatures before Allāh.'"[1]

They combine the two evils; worshipping at the graves and making graven images and statues." [2]

1 — Al-Bukhārī: (434), Muslim: (528)

2 — This a statement from Ibn al-Qayyim in *Ighāthatu al-Lahfān*: (1/184). A similar statement is found in *al-Iqtiḍā* of Ibn Taymiyyah: (2/679).

وَلَهُمَا عَنْهَا(رَضِيَ اللَّهُ عَنْهَا) ، قَالَتْ: «لَمَّا نُزِلَ بِرَسُولِ اللهِ صَلَّى اللَّهُ عَلَيْهِ وَسَلَّمَ طَفِقَ يَطْرَحُ خَمِيصَةً لَهُ عَلَى وَجْهِهِ، فَإِذَا اغْتَمَّ بِهَا كَشَفَهَا، فَقَالَ - وَهُوَ كَذَلِكَ -: «لَعَنَةُ اللهُ عَلَى الْيَهُودِ وَالنَّصَارَى، اتَّخَذُوا قُبُورَ أَنْبِيَائِهِمْ مَسَاجِدَ»؛ يُحَذِّرُ مَا صَنَعُوا، وَلَوْلَا ذَلِكَ لأُبْرِزَ قَبْرُهُ، غَيْرَ أَنَّهُ خُشِيَ أَنْ يُتَّخَذَ مَسْجِدًا». أَخْرَجَاهُ.

Also, in Al-Bukhārī and Muslim, it is reported that `Aishah (رَضِيَ اللَّهُ عَنْهَا) narrated: "When death approached Allāh's Messenger (صَلَّى اللَّهُ عَلَيْهِ وَسَلَّمَ) he began to draw a piece of cloth (bed sheet) over his face, (sometimes covering and sometimes removing it out of distress), he (صَلَّى اللَّهُ عَلَيْهِ وَسَلَّمَ) said in this state: 'Allāh's curse be upon the Jews and the Christians for taking the graves of their Prophets as places of worship' — warning the people about their actions. If he did not fear the making the Prophet's grave a place of worship, his (صَلَّى اللَّهُ عَلَيْهِ وَسَلَّمَ) grave would have been as open as the graves of his companions (رَضِيَ اللَّهُ عَنْهُمْ)." (Al-Bukhārī and Muslim)[1]

1 — Al-Bukhārī: (435,1330 and 1390), Muslim: (531).

وَلِمُسْلِمٍ عَنْ جُنْدَبِ بْنِ عَبْدِ اللهِ، قَالَ: سَمِعْتُ النَّبِيَّ ﷺ قَبْلَ أَنْ يَمُوتَ بِخَمْسٍ، وَهُوَ يَقُولُ: «إِنِّي أَبْرَأُ إِلَى اللهِ أَنْ يَكُونَ لِي مِنْكُمْ خَلِيلٌ؛ فَإِنَّ اللهَ قَدِ اتَّخَذَنِي خَلِيلًا، كَمَا اتَّخَذَ إِبْرَاهِيمَ خَلِيلًا، وَلَوْ كُنْتُ مُتَّخِذًا مِنْ أُمَّتِي خَلِيلًا؛ لَاتَّخَذْتُ أَبَا بَكْرٍ خَلِيلًا، أَلَا وَإِنَّ مَنْ كَانَ قَبْلَكُمْ كَانُوا يَتَّخِذُونَ قُبُورَ أَنْبِيَائِهِمْ مَسَاجِدَ، أَلَا فَلَا تَتَّخِذُوا الْقُبُورَ مَسَاجِدَ، فَإِنِّي أَنْهَاكُمْ عَنْ ذَلِكَ».

Muslim reported that Jundub b. 'Abdullāh (رضي الله عنه) narrated: I heard the Prophet (ﷺ) say five days before his death: "I am free and clear towards Allāh of having any of you as my Khalīl (especially close friend). Verily, Allāh has taken me as His Khalīl just as He had taken Ibrāhīm (ﷺ) as a Khalīl. If I was to take anyone from my Ummah as a Khalīl, I would have taken Abū Bakr (رضي الله عنه) as a Khalīl. Beware! Those who came before you took their Prophets' graves as places of worship. Beware! Do not take graves as places of worship. I forbid you to do so."[1]

1 — Muslim: (532)

فَقَدْ نَهَى عَنْهُ فِي آخِرِ حَيَاتِهِ، ثُمَّ إِنَّهُ لَعَنَ - وَهُوَ فِي السِّيَاقِ - مَنْ فَعَلَهُ، وَالصَّلَاةُ عِنْدَهَا مِنْ ذَلِكَ، وَإِنْ لَمْ يُبْنَ مَسْجِدٌ؛ وَهُوَ مَعْنَى قَوْلِهَا: «خَشِيَ أَنْ يُتَّخَذَ مَسْجِدًا»، فَإِنَّ الصَّحَابَةَ رَضِيَ اللَّهُ عَنْهُمْ لَمْ يَكُونُوا لِيَبْنُوا حَوْلَ قَبْرِهِ مَسْجِدًا. وَكُلُّ مَوْضِعٍ قُصِدَتِ الصَّلَاةُ فِيهِ فَقَدِ اتُّخِذَ مَسْجِدًا، بَلْ كُلُّ مَوْضِعٍ يُصَلَّى فِيهِ يُسَمَّى مَسْجِدًا، كَمَا قَالَ صَلَّى اللَّهُ عَلَيْهِ وَسَلَّمَ: «جُعِلَتْ لِيَ الأَرْضُ مَسْجِدًا وَطَهُورًا».

He (صَلَّى اللَّهُ عَلَيْهِ وَسَلَّمَ) forbade this at the end of his life. After this, he cursed anyone who did any such deed within this context. Prayer at the graves is one of these deeds, even if no Masjid has been built. This is the meaning of ʿĀishah's (رَضِيَ اللَّهُ عَنْهَا) statement "He feared (his grave) would be taken as a Masjid." The companions never built any place of worship around his grave. Any place which is intended for prayer or where the prayer is performed has indeed been taken as a Masjid. Just as the Prophet (صَلَّى اللَّهُ عَلَيْهِ وَسَلَّمَ) said: "The whole earth has been made for me a Masjid and it is pure and clean."[1]

1 — Al-Bukhārī: (330), Muslim: (521) narrated by Jābir b. ʿAbdullāh (رَضِيَ اللَّهُ عَنْهُمَا).

وَلِأَحْمَدَ - بِسَنَدٍ جَيِّدٍ - عَنِ ابْنِ مَسْعُودٍ رَضِيَ اللَّهُ عَنْهُ مَرْفُوعًا: «إِنَّ مِنْ شِرَارِ النَّاسِ مَنْ تُدْرِكُهُمُ السَّاعَةُ وَهُمْ أَحْيَاءٌ، وَالَّذِينَ يَتَّخِذُونَ الْقُبُورَ مَسَاجِدَ». رَوَاهُ أَبُو حَاتِمٍ فِي صَحِيحِهِ.

Aḥmad has reported with a good sanad (chain) that Ibn Mas'ūd (رَضِيَ اللَّهُ عَنْهُ) narrated in a Marfū' ḥadīth: "The evilest men are those upon whom the last Hour comes while they are still alive, and those who take graves as places of worship (Masājid)". This ḥadīth was also reported by Abū Ḥātim in his *Ṣaḥiḥ*.[1]

1 — *Ṣaḥiḥ ibn Ḥibbān*: (6847), al-Musnad: (7/394). Ibn Taymiyyah in *al-Iqtiḍā*: (3/674) and Sh.al-Albānī: *Taḥdhīr as-Sājid*: (18-19) declared this chain as good. In the chain is a narrator called 'Āṣim b. Abī Najūd who has been criticized for his memory [*al-Jarḥ wa at-Ta'dīl*: (6/341)]. Therefore, that which can be understood from the previous mentioned statements of the scholars of ḥadīth is that this narration is ḥasan (acceptable). This is due to 'Āṣim's presence in the chain.

ISSUES OF THIS CHAPTER:

1. That (threat) which was mentioned by Allāh's Messenger (صَلَّى ٱللَّهُ عَلَيْهِ وَسَلَّمَ) over the one who builds a mosque to worship Allāh near the grave of a righteous person even with good intention.

2. Prohibition of statues and their likenesses and the gravity of the matter.

3. A lesson in the emphasis of the Prophet (صَلَّى ٱللَّهُ عَلَيْهِ وَسَلَّمَ) on this. How he first explained and clarified the issue (politely), then five days before his death saying what he said, then at the time of his death, that which was previously said was insufficient (so he repeated he statement صَلَّى ٱللَّهُ عَلَيْهِ وَسَلَّمَ).

4. The Prophet (صَلَّى ٱللَّهُ عَلَيْهِ وَسَلَّمَ) strongly prohibited the turning of his grave into a Masjid before it had even come into existence.

5. It was the practice of the Jews and the Christians to turn the graves of their Prophets into places of worship.

6. His curse on the Jews and Christians for this practice.

7. His intention in doing so was to warn us regarding his grave.

8. The reason for not raising his grave.

9. The meaning of taking them (graves) as places of worship.

10. The Prophet (صَلَّى ٱللَّهُ عَلَيْهِ وَسَلَّمَ) linked those who took the graves as Masjid to those upon whom the Hour will occur. He mentioned the means to Shirk before its actual occurrence along with its final consequence.

11. The mentioning of the Prophet (صَلَّى ٱللَّهُ عَلَيْهِ وَسَلَّمَ) in his speech is a refutation of the two worst sects of innovators just five days before his death. Some scholars have not included these two sects in the 72 sects. These two sects are the Rāfidah and Jahmiyah.

    The occurrence of Shirk and grave worshipping was due to the Rafidah sect, and they were the first to build Masajid over graves.

12. The suffering of the Prophet (صَلَّى ٱللَّهُ عَلَيْهِ وَسَلَّمَ) with pains and affliction from the agony of death.

13. Allāh awarded the favor of making him a Khalil (friend).

14. A clear declaration that close friendship is more valuable than love.

ISSUES OF THIS CHAPTER:

15. A clear declaration that As-Siddiq (Abū Bakr) (رَضِيَٱللَّهُعَنْهُ) was the best of the Companions.

16. The indication to him (Abū Bakr) as a caliph, a successor to the Prophet (صَلَّىٱللَّهُعَلَيْهِوَسَلَّمَ).

CHAPTER EXERCISES

1. What was the norm of those before from Christians and Jews regarding the graves of those they deemed pious?

2. What does Marfū' mean?

3. How does the author implement al-Qiyās al-awlā (analogy of the superior) in this chapter?

4. In the ḥadīth of Ibn Mas'ūd (رَضِيَ ٱللَّهُ عَنْهُ), what are the examples of two of the most evil people?

5. What is the meaning of Masjid?

CHAPTER EXERCISES

CHAPTER EXERCISES

Page 206

CHAPTER 20:

Exaggeration of Righteous People's Graves Leads to them Being idols Worshipped besides Allāh

رَوَى مَالِكٌ فِي الْمُوطَّأِ؛ أَنَّ رَسُولَ اللهِ صَلَّى اللهُ عَلَيْهِ وَسَلَّمَ قَالَ: «اللَّهُمَّ لَا تَجْعَلْ قَبْرِي وَثَنًا يُعْبَدُ، اشْتَدَّ غَضَبُ اللهِ عَلَى قَوْمٍ اتَّخَذُوا قُبُورَ أَنْبِيَائِهِمْ مَسَاجِدَ».

Imām Mālik recorded in his al-Muwaṭṭa' that the Messenger of Allāh (صَلَّى اللهُ عَلَيْهِ وَسَلَّمَ) said: "O Allāh! Never turn my grave into an idol to be worshipped. Allāh's wrath intensified on a people who turned their Prophet's graves into places of worship."[1]

1 — *Al-Muwaṭṭa'*: (570) the Abī Muṣ'ab copy. *Kashf al-Astār*: (1/220 no.440) Authenticated by Sh. Al-Albānī in *Taḥdhīr as-Sājid*: (17-18),

وَلِابْنِ جَرِيرٍ بِسَنَدِهِ عَنْ سُفْيَانَ، عَنْ مَنْصُورٍ، عَنْ مُجَاهِدٍ: ﴿أَفَرَأَيْتُمُ اللَّاتَ وَالْعُزَّىٰ﴾، قَالَ: «كَانَ يَلُتُّ لَهُمُ السَّوِيقَ فَمَاتَ، فَعَكَفُوا عَلَى قَبْرِهِ». وَكَذَا قَالَ أَبُو الْجَوْزَاءِ، عَنِ ابْنِ عَبَّاسٍ رَضِيَ اللَّهُ عَنْهُمَا: «كَانَ يَلُتُّ السَّوِيقَ لِلْحَاجِّ».

Ibn Jarīr reported from Sufyān, from Mansūr, that Mujāhid said concerning the verse; *"Have you then considered Al-Lat and Al-Uzza" [53:19]*: "He (Lāt) used to serve Sawīq[1] for them. Once he died, the people began to religiously confine at his grave."[2]

Abul-Jawzā likewise reported from Ibn Abbās (رَضِيَ اللَّهُ عَنْهُمَا): "He (Lāt) used to serve Sawīq for pilgrims."[3]

1 — Fine flour of barley or wheat mixed with water and ghee.

2 — *Tafsīr aṭ-Ṭabarī*: (22/47-48).

3 — Al-Bukhārī: (4859).

وَعَـنِ ابْـنِ عَبَّـاسٍ رَضِيَٱللَّهُعَنْهُمَا قَـالَ: «لَعَـنَ رَسُـولُ اللـهِ صَلَّىٱللَّهُعَلَيْهِوَسَلَّمَ زَائِـرَاتِ الْقُبُـورِ، وَالْمُتَّخِذِيـنَ عَلَيْهَـا الْمَسَـاجِدَ وَالسُّـرُجَ». رَوَاهُ أَهْـلُ السُّـنَنِ.

Ibn Abbās (رَضِيَٱللَّهُعَنْهُمَا) reported: "Allāh's Messenger (صَلَّىٱللَّهُعَلَيْهِوَسَلَّمَ) cursed the women who visit graves. He (صَلَّىٱللَّهُعَلَيْهِوَسَلَّمَ) also cursed those who set up mosques and lights over graves." [This Hadith has been collected by Abū Dāwūd, At-Tirmidhī, Ibn Mājah, and An-Nasā'ī].[1]

1 — *Al-Musnad*: (3/471), At-Tirmidhī: (320), An-Nasāī [*aṣ-Ṣughrā*]: (2043), An-Nasāī [*al-Kubrā*]: (2181) Abū Dāwūd: (3236). Authenticated by Shaykh al-Islām ibn Taymiyyah: (31/206) and Sh. Aḥmad Shākir: (3/323).

ISSUES OF THIS CHAPTER:

1. Explanation of idols.
2. Explanation of worship.
3. The Prophet (صَلَّى ٱللَّٰهُ عَلَيْهِ وَسَلَّمَ) did not seek refuge in Allāh except from that which he feared would occur.
4. The Prophet's (صَلَّى ٱللَّٰهُ عَلَيْهِ وَسَلَّمَ) joining this supplication i.e. "O Allāh! Never turn my grave..." with taking the graves of Prophets as Masjid.
5. Mention of the intense wrath of Allāh (on those who fall into such practices).
6. Of most importance is the description as to how the worship of al-Lāt, one of the major (pre-Islamic) idols, was started.
7. The knowledge that al-Lāt was the grave of a righteous man.
8. Al-Lāt was the name of a person buried in that grave and the mention of the meaning behind (the idol) being given that name.
9. Curse (of the Prophet صَلَّى ٱللَّٰهُ عَلَيْهِ وَسَلَّمَ) on the women who visit the graves.
10. The Prophet's (صَلَّى ٱللَّٰهُ عَلَيْهِ وَسَلَّمَ) curse upon those who put up lights and ornaments on the graves.

CHAPTER EXERCISES

1. What is the meaning of 'exaggeration' (الغلو)?
2. Where are the words 'al-Lāt' and 'al-'Uzzah' derived from?
3. Where in this chapter can we find examples of how idol worshippers dishonored Allāh's names?
4. Where in this chapter is an example of the protectiveness of the Messenger (صَلَّى ٱللَّهُ عَلَيْهِ وَسَلَّمَ) of at-Tawḥīd?
5. What is the wisdom behind the prohibition on exaggerating the praise of individuals?

CHAPTER EXERCISES

CHAPTER EXERCISES

CHAPTER EXERCISES

CHAPTER 21:

The Protectiveness of Al-Mustafa (صَلَّى ٱللَّهُ عَلَيْهِ وَسَلَّمَ) of Tawhid and his Blocking of Paths Leading to Shirk

وَقَوْلِ اللهِ تَعَالَى: ﴿لَقَدْ جَاءَكُمْ رَسُولٌ مِّنْ أَنفُسِكُمْ عَزِيزٌ عَلَيْهِ مَا عَنِتُّمْ﴾... الآيَةَ.

عَنْ أَبِي هُرَيْرَةَ رَضِيَ ٱللَّهُ عَنْهُ قَالَ: قَالَ رَسُولُ اللهِ صَلَّى ٱللَّهُ عَلَيْهِ وَسَلَّمَ: «لَا تَجْعَلُوا بُيُوتَكُمْ قُبُورًا، وَلَا تَجْعَلُوا قَبْرِي عِيدًا، وَصَلُّوا عَلَيَّ؛ فَإِنَّ صَلَاتَكُمْ تَبْلُغُنِي حَيْثُ كُنْتُمْ». رَوَاهُ أَبُو دَاوُدَ بِإِسْنَادٍ حَسَنٍ، وَرُوَاتُهُ ثِقَاتٌ.

Allāh the Most Exalted said: "Verily, there has come to you a Messenger from amongst yourselves it grieves him that you should receive any injury or difficulty." [9:128] Until the end of the verse...

Abū Hurayrah (رَضِيَ ٱللَّهُ عَنْهُ) narrated that Allāh's Messenger (صَلَّى ٱللَّهُ عَلَيْهِ وَسَلَّمَ) said: "Do not make your home graves. Do not make my grave a place of celebration. Send your Salat (blessings, graces, honors, and mercy) on me. Your Salat will be conveyed to me, wherever you may be." [Abū Dāwūd recorded this Hadith with a reliable chain of narrators].[1]

1 — *Al-Musnad*: (14/403), Abū Dāwūd: (2042), Authenticated by An-Nawawī in *Al-Adhkār*: (203)

وعَنْ عَلِيِّ بْنِ الْحُسَيْنِ رَضِيَ ٱللَّهُ عَنْهُمَا؛ أَنَّهُ رَأَى رَجُلًا يَجِيءُ إِلَى فُرْجَةٍ كَانَتْ عِنْدَ قَبْرِ النَّبِيِّ صَلَّى ٱللَّهُ عَلَيْهِ وَسَلَّمَ، فَيَدْخُلُ فِيهَا فَيَدْعُو، فنهَاهُ، وَقَالَ: أَلَا أُحَدِّثُكُمْ حَدِيثًا سَمِعْتُهُ مِنْ أَبِي، عَنْ جَدِّي، عَنْ رَسُولِ اللهِ صَلَّى ٱللَّهُ عَلَيْهِ وَسَلَّمَ قَالَ: «لَا تَتَّخِذُوا قَبْرِي عِيدًا، وَلَا بُيُوتَكُمْ قُبُورًا؛ فَإِنَّ تَسْلِيمَكُمْ يَبْلُغُنِي أَيْنَ كُنْتُمْ». رَوَاهُ فِي الْمُخْتَارَةِ

And ʿAlī b. Ḥusayn (رَضِيَ ٱللَّهُ عَنْهُمَا) narrated: He saw a man at a space that was at the grave of the Prophet (صَلَّى ٱللَّهُ عَلَيْهِ وَسَلَّمَ) and he would go in it and supplicate. So he prevented the man and instructed him saying, "Should I not tell you a hadith which I heard from my father who in turn heard it from my grandfather (رَضِيَ ٱللَّهُ عَنْهُ) that Allāh's Messenger (صَلَّى ٱللَّهُ عَلَيْهِ وَسَلَّمَ) said: 'Do not take my grave as a place of celebration, nor your homes as graves, make Salat (blessing, graces, honors, and mercy) upon me, for, your salutation (asking safety for me) will be conveyed to me from wherever you are.'" [*Al-Mukhtārah*][1]

1 — *Al-Mukhtārah*: (2/49 no.428), *Muṣannaf Ibn Abī Shaybah*: (7624). As-Sakhāwī classified this narration as ḥasan (acceptable). Sh. Al-Albānī authenticated it in *Taḥdhīr as-Sājid*: (95) grading it as ṣaḥīḥ [through external support from other narrations].

ISSUES OF THIS CHAPTER:

1. Explanation of the verses in Surah Bara'ah (Taubah).
2. The Prophet (صَلَّى ٱللَّهُ عَلَيْهِ وَسَلَّمَ) did his best to keep his Ummah far away from the boundaries of Shirk as far as possible.
3. The Prophet's (صَلَّى ٱللَّهُ عَلَيْهِ وَسَلَّمَ) concern for our well-being and success and his compassion and mercy.
4. The Prophet (صَلَّى ٱللَّهُ عَلَيْهِ وَسَلَّمَ) forbade visiting his grave in a certain manner, though visiting his grave is among the best of deeds (it reminds one of the Hereafter).
5. The Prophet (صَلَّى ٱللَّهُ عَلَيْهِ وَسَلَّمَ) forbade us to make excessive visits to his grave.
6. His encouragement to perform voluntary prayers at home.
7. It is established among the Companions (رَضِيَ ٱللَّهُ عَنْهُمْ) that offering Salat in the cemetery is prohibited.
8. The explanation that a person's invocation of Salat (blessings, graces, honors, and mercy) and Salam upon the Prophet (صَلَّى ٱللَّهُ عَلَيْهِ وَسَلَّمَ) is conveyed to him even if he may be far away. So there is no evidence for those who deem it a necessity to be close to his grave.
9. He (صَلَّى ٱللَّهُ عَلَيْهِ وَسَلَّمَ) is in Al-Barzakh where the Salat and Salam of his Ummah are conveyed (to him).

CHAPTER EXERCISES

1. What are some examples of prohibited celebrations ('Īd)?

2. Which narration in this chapter further emphasizes the virtues of praying non-obligatory prayers at home?

3. Mention some of the characteristics of the final Messenger Muḥammad (صَلَّى ٱللَّهُ عَلَيْهِ وَسَلَّمَ) mentioned in this chapter?

4. What is the link between this chapter and the previous chapter?

5. What is the proof in this chapter for the prohibition of excessively frequenting the grave of the Prophet (صَلَّى ٱللَّهُ عَلَيْهِ وَسَلَّمَ) to give salutations upon him?

CHAPTER EXERCISES

CHAPTER EXERCISES

CHAPTER 22:

Some People of this Ummah (Nation) will worship Idols

وَقَوْلُ اللهِ تَعَالَى: ﴿أَلَمْ تَرَ إِلَى الَّذِينَ أُوتُوا نَصِيبًا مِّنَ الْكِتَابِ يُؤْمِنُونَ بِالْجِبْتِ وَالطَّاغُوتِ﴾ النساء: ٥١

وَقَوْلُ اللهِ تَعَالَى : ﴿قُلْ هَلْ أُنَبِّئُكُم بِشَرٍّ مِّن ذَٰلِكَ مَثُوبَةً عِندَ اللَّهِ ۚ مَن لَّعَنَهُ اللَّهُ وَغَضِبَ عَلَيْهِ وَجَعَلَ مِنْهُمُ الْقِرَدَةَ وَالْخَنَازِيرَ وَعَبَدَ الطَّاغُوتَ﴾ المائدة: ٦٠

Allāh the Almighty said: "Have you not seen those who were given a portion of the Scripture? They believe in *Al-Jibt* and *At-Ṭāghūt* (all false deities)." [4:51]

Allāh the Almighty said: "Say: Shall I inform you of something worse than that, regarding the recompense from Allāh: those who incurred the curse of Allāh and His wrath. Some of them He turned into monkeys and swine, and some worshipped Ṭāghūt (false deities)." [5:60]

وَقَوْلُهُ: ﴿قَالَ الَّذِينَ غَلَبُوا عَلَىٰ أَمْرِهِمْ لَنَتَّخِذَنَّ عَلَيْهِم مَّسْجِدًا﴾ الكهف: ٢١

عَـنْ أَبِـي سَـعِيدٍ رَضِيَٱللَّهُعَنْهُ؛ أَنَّ رَسُـولَ اللـهِ صَلَّىٱللَّهُعَلَيْهِوَسَلَّمَ قَـالَ: «لَتَتَّبِعُـنَّ سَـنَنَ مَـنْ كَانَ قَبْلَكُـمْ، حَـذْوَ الْقُـذَّةِ بِالْقُـذَّةِ، حَتَّـى لَـوْ دَخَلُـوا جُحْرَ ضَـبٍّ لَدَخَلْتُمُـوهُ»، قَالُـوا: يَـا رَسُـولَ اللـهِ، الْيَهُـودَ وَالنَّصَـارَى؟ قَـالَ: «فَمَـنْ؟!». أَخْرَجَـاهُ.

He, Allāh said: "Those who prevailed in the matter said: 'We verily shall build a place of worship over them.'" [18:21]

Abū Sa'īd (رَضِيَٱللَّهُعَنْهُ) narrated that the Prophet (صَلَّىٱللَّهُعَلَيْهِوَسَلَّمَ) said: "You will surely follow the ways of those who came before you, in everything as one arrow would to another, so much so that even if they entered a sand lizard's hole, you would enter it too." They said, "O Allāh's Messenger! Do you mean to say that we will follow the Jews and the Christians?" He replied (صَلَّىٱللَّهُعَلَيْهِوَسَلَّمَ), "Who else?" (Al-Bukhārī and Muslim)[1]

1 — Al-Bukhārī: (3456), Muslim: (2669). The wording used by the author (رَحِمَهُٱللَّهُ) is the same meaning found in two authentic compilations.

وَلِمُسْلِمٍ عَنْ ثَوْبَانَ رَضِيَ اللَّهُ عَنْهُ، أَنَّ رَسُولَ اللهِ صَلَّى اللَّهُ عَلَيْهِ وَسَلَّمَ قَالَ: «إِنَّ اللهَ زَوَى لِيَ الأَرْضَ فَرَأَيْتُ مَشَارِقَهَا وَمَغَارِبَهَا، وَإِنَّ أُمَّتِي سَيَبْلُغُ مُلْكُهَا مَا زُوِيَ لِي مِنْهَا، وَأُعْطِيتُ الْكَنْزَيْنِ: الأَحْمَرَ وَالأَبْيَضَ، وَإِنِّي سَأَلْتُ رَبِّي لِأُمَّتِي أَنْ لَا يُهْلِكَهَا بِسَنَةٍ بِعَامَّةٍ، وَأَنْ لَا يُسَلِّطَ عَلَيْهِمْ عَدُوًّا مِنْ سِوَى أَنْفُسِهِمْ، فَيَسْتَبِيحَ بَيْضَتَهُمْ...

Muslim reported from Thawbān (رَضِيَ اللَّهُ عَنْهُ) that Allāh's Messenger (صَلَّى اللَّهُ عَلَيْهِ وَسَلَّمَ) said: "Allāh the Most Exalted gathered the earth for me, that I saw its east and west. Verily my Ummah's authority shall reach over all that was shown to me of it. And I have been granted the two treasures; the red and the white. I asked my Lord that my Ummah not be destroyed by a universal drought, and not to let others have control over them from their enemies to annihilate them...

> وَإِنَّ رَبِّي قَالَ: يَا مُحَمَّدُ، إِذَا قَضَيْتُ قَضَاءً فَإِنَّهُ لَا يُرَدُّ، وَإِنِّي أَعْطَيْتُكَ لِأُمَّتِكَ أَنْ لَا أُهْلِكَهَا بِسَنَةٍ بِعَامَّةٍ، وَأَنْ لَا أُسَلِّطَ عَلَيْهِمْ عَدُوًّا مِنْ سِوَى أَنْفُسِهِمْ فَيَسْتَبِيحَ بَيْضَتَهُمْ، وَلَوِ اجْتَمَعَ عَلَيْهِمْ مَنْ بِأَقْطَارِهَا، حَتَّى يَكُونَ بَعْضُهُمْ يُهْلِكُ بَعْضًا، وَيَسْبِيَ بَعْضُهُمْ بَعْضًا».
>
> ...My Lord said: 'O Muḥammad! When I issue a decree, it is not reversed. I have granted for your Ummah that they shall not be destroyed by universal drought. And that they will not be overcome by enemies outside of themselves reaching to their heart of power-even if they gather against them from all regions; only a section of them will destroy another section, and a section will take as prisoner another section.'"[1]

1 — Muslim: (2889)

وَرَوَاهُ الْبَرْقَانِيُّ فِي صَحِيحِهِ، وَزَادَ: «وَإِنَّمَا أَخَافُ عَلَى أُمَّتِي الأَئِمَّةَ الْمُضِلِّينَ، وَإِذَا وَقَعَ عَلَيْهِمُ السَّيْفُ لَمْ يُرْفَعْ إِلَى يَوْمِ الْقِيَامَةِ، وَلَا تَقُومُ السَّاعَةُ حَتَّى يَلْحَقَ حَيٌّ مِنْ أُمَّتِي بِالْمُشْرِكِينَ، وَحَتَّى تَعْبُدَ فِئَامٌ مِنْ أُمَّتِي الأَوْثَانَ...

Al-Barqānī recorded this ḥadīth in his *Ṣaḥiḥ*[1] and added to it the following words; "That which I fear for my Ummah are those heads that will lead others astray. When the sword is used amongst my people, it will not be lifted from them until the Day of Resurrection, and the Last Hour will not come until the tribes of my people will attach themselves to the polytheists and until large groups of my people will worship idols...

1 — Al-Barqānī — he is; Abū Bakr b. Aḥmad b. Muḥammad al-Khuwārazmī a scholar of ḥadīth died 425h (see *Siyar A'alām an-Nubalā*: 17/464). The majority of the book *Ṣaḥīḥ of Al-Barqānī* mentioned here by the author is lost including this reference. However, this ḥadīth has been compiled by others. This is mentioned in the following footnote.

وَإِنَّهُ سَيَكُونُ فِي أُمَّتِي كَذَّابُونَ ثَلَاثُونَ كُلُّهُمْ يَزْعُمُ أَنَّهُ نَبِيٌّ، وَأَنَا خَاتَمُ النَّبِيِّينَ، لَا نَبِيَّ بَعْدِي، وَلَا تَزَالُ طَائِفَةٌ مِنْ أُمَّتِي عَلَى الْحَقِّ مَنْصُورَةً، لَا يَضُرُّهُمْ مَنْ خَذَلَهُمْ حَتَّى يَأْتِيَ أَمْرُ اللهِ تَبَارَكَ وَتَعَالَى».

...There will be in my ummah thirty great liars; each of them claiming that he is a prophet, whereas I am the finality of the Prophets. There will be no Prophet after me; There will never cease to be a group from my ummah firm upon the truth and victorious. They will not be harmed by those who forsake them until Allāh's Command comes."[1]

1 — *Al-Musnad*: (37/78), Abū Dāwūd: (4252). Authenticated by al-Ḥākim in his *al-Mustadrak*: (4/449), Ibn Ḥibbān in his *Ṣaḥīḥ*: (16/220 no.7238) and Sh. al-Albānī: (*Ṣaḥīḥ al-Jāmi'*: (1/365 no.1769).

ISSUES OF THIS CHAPTER:

1. Explanation of the verse in An-Nisa' (4:5).

2. Explanation of the verse in Al-Ma'idah (5:60).

3. Explanation of the verse in Al-Kahf (18:21).

4. The most important issue is what is meant by believing in Al-Jibt (magic, Shirk, idols) and At-Ṭāghūt (all false deities worshipped besides Allāh). Does it mean believing in that sincerely by the heart; or approval of those who do so while hating it and knowing its falsehood?

5. Their (Jews) saying (regarding the pagan Quraish) that the disbelievers who are well aware of their Kufr (disbelief) are on a more correct and guided path than the believers.

6. Such people are in the Muslim community (the Ummah) as is proven by the Ḥadīth of Abū Sa'id Al-Khudrī (رَضِيَ اللَّهُ عَنْهُ). This is the main objective of the Chapter.

7. The occurrence of his declaration that many followers of this Ummah will worship false deities.

8. Most amazing is the appearance of those claiming Prophethood, like Al-Mukhtar, despite his proclamation of *Ash-Shahadatain*, and his declaration of being a part of this Ummah, and (his testifying) that the Messenger [Muḥammad صَلَّى اللَّهُ عَلَيْهِ وَسَلَّمَ] was true and the Qur'ān was true and therein is the confirmation that Muḥammad (رَضِيَ اللَّهُ عَنْهُ) was the "Seal" of the Prophets. He was believed despite his clear and open contradiction to it (*Ash-Shahadatain*). Al-Mukhtar appeared in the latter era of the Companions and many people followed him.

9. The glad tiding that the truth will never perish completely as it had in the past. Indeed, there will always be a group upon the truth.

10. The greatest of signs is that they (the victorious group) will not be harmed by those who oppose them and fight against them despite (them) being few.

11. This will be the case until the Last Hour.

12. There are several signs in the statement of the Prophet (صَلَّى ٱللَّهُ عَلَيْهِ وَسَلَّمَ)

- Allāh folded for him (صَلَّى ٱللَّهُ عَلَيْهِ وَسَلَّمَ) the east and the west (i.e. the lands under the control of Islam); the meaning of it; and that it indeed occurred as he informed; as opposed to the north and the south.
- That two treasures (i.e. treasures of Rome and Persia) were bestowed upon him.
- That two of his invocations on behalf of his nation have been accepted.
- That the third of his invocations was prevented.
- That the sword would be used and that it would not be lifted after that.
- That false prophets would appear among this nation (the Muslims).
- There would always be a victorious group.
- All of this occurred as he mentioned even though each one of them was far from what could have been conceived.

13. The extent of his fear for his nation (صَلَّى ٱللَّهُ عَلَيْهِ وَسَلَّمَ) from the misguided and astray leaders.

14. Warning and emphasis on the meaning of idol worship.

CHAPTER EXERCISES

1. What is the meaning of ṭāghūt?
2. Where in this chapter is the proof for the impermissibility of imitating the Jews and Christians?
3. Identify where the proof that Muḥammad (ﷺ) is the seal of the Prophets?
4. Who are the victorious group? What are their characteristics?
5. What is the relevance of this chapter to Kitāb At-Tawḥīd?

CHAPTER EXERCISES

CHAPTER EXERCISES

CHAPTER EXERCISES

Page 232

CHAPTER 23:

The Chapter on Sorcery and Magic

وَقَوْلِ اللهِ تَعَالَى: ﴿وَلَقَدْ عَلِمُوا لَمَنِ اشْتَرَاهُ مَا لَهُ فِي الْآخِرَةِ مِنْ خَلَاقٍ﴾ البقرة: ١٠٢ وَقَوْلُهُ: ﴿يُؤْمِنُونَ بِالْجِبْتِ وَالطَّاغُوتِ﴾ النساء: ٥١

قَالَ عُمَرُ رَضِيَ اللَّهُ عَنْهُ: «الجِبتُ: السِّحْرُ، وَالطَّاغُوتُ: الشَّيْطَانُ». وَقَالَ جَابِرٌ رَضِيَ اللَّهُ عَنْهُ: «الطَّوَاغِيتُ: كُهَّانٌ كَانَ يَنْزِلُ عَلَيْهِمُ الشَّيْطَانُ، فِي كُلِّ حَيٍّ وَاحِدٌ».

Allāh the Most Exalted said: "And indeed they knew that the buyers of it (magic) would have no share in the Hereafter." [2:102] And he said: "They believe in Al-Jibt and At-Ṭāghūt (all false deities)." [4:51]

'Umar (رَضِيَ اللَّهُ عَنْهُ) said that Al-Jibt is magic (sorcery) while At-Ṭāghūt is Ash-Shayṭān.[1] And Jābir (رَضِيَ اللَّهُ عَنْهُ) said that At-Ṭāghūt are soothsayers upon whom the devil descends and every tribe has one.[2]

1 — This is found in a suspended chain (Mu'allaq) in Al-Bukhārī: (6/45) with a chain that has been declared strong by al-Ḥāfiẓ ibn Ḥajr in *Fatḥ Al-Bārī* (8/252 – Dār al-M'arifah print). The chain (isnad) is connected in *Sunan Sa'īd b. Mansūr* (2534).

2 — This is found in a suspended chain (Mu'allaq) in Al-Bukhārī: (6/45). The chain (isnad) is connected in *Tafsīr at-Ṭabarī*: (4/558).

عَـنْ أَبِـي هُرَيْـرَةَ رَضِيَ اللَّهُ عَنْهُ؛ أَنَّ رَسُـولَ اللهِ صَلَّى اللَّهُ عَلَيْهِ وَسَلَّمَ قَـالَ: «اجْتَنِبُـوا السَّـبْعَ الْمُوبِقَـاتِ»، قَالُـوا: يَـا رَسُـولَ اللهِ، وَمَـا هُـنَّ؟ قَـالَ: «الشِّـرْكُ بِاللهِ، وَالسِّـحْرُ، وَقَتْـلُ النَّفْـسِ الَّتِـي حَـرَّمَ اللهُ إِلَّا بِالْحَـقِّ، وَأَكْلُ الرِّبَـا، وَأَكْلُ مَـالِ الْيَتِيـمِ، وَالتَّوَلِّـي يَـوْمَ الزَّحْـفِ، وَقَـذْفُ الْمُحْصَنَـاتِ الْغَـافِلَاتِ الْمُؤْمِنَـاتِ».

Abū Hurayrah (رَضِيَ اللَّهُ عَنْهُ) is reported that the Prophet (صَلَّى اللَّهُ عَلَيْهِ وَسَلَّمَ) said: "Save yourself from the seven destroyers." They (رَضِيَ اللَّهُ عَنْهُمْ) asked: "O Messenger of Allāh, what are they?" He (صَلَّى اللَّهُ عَلَيْهِ وَسَلَّمَ) said, "To associate partners with Allāh, sorcery, killing a life Allāh has forbidden to kill, taking usury, stealing or wasting the wealth of orphans, turning your back at the battlefield, and making an accusation against chaste, unmindful women."[1]

1 — Al-Bukhārī: (2766), Muslim: (89)

وَعَنْ جُنْدَبٍ مَرْفُوعًا: «حَدُّ السَّاحِرِ: ضَرْبُهُ بِالسَّيْفِ». رَوَاهُ التِّرْمِذِيُّ، وَقَالَ: «الصَّحِيحُ أَنَّهُ مَوْقُوفٌ».
وَفِي صَحِيحِ الْبُخَارِيِّ عَنْ بَجَالَةَ بْنِ عَبَدَةَ قَالَ: كَتَبَ عُمَرُ بْنُ الْخَطَّابِ : أَنِ اقْتُلُوا كُلَّ سَاحِرٍ وَسَاحِرَةٍ،
قَالَ: فَقَتَلْنَا ثَلَاثَ سَوَاحِرَ. وَصَحَّ عَنْ حَفْصَةَ أَنَّهَا أَمَرَتْ بِقَتْلِ جَارِيَةٍ لَهَا سَحَرَتْهَا، فَقُتِلَتْ. وَكَذَا صَحَّ
عَنْ جُنْدَبٍ . قَالَ أَحْمَدُ: «عَنْ ثَلَاثَةٍ مِنْ أَصْحَابِ رَسُولِ اللهِ ».

Jundub (رَضِيَ اللَّهُ عَنْهُ) narrated the following Marfū' Hadith, which At-Tirmidhī reported who said that which is correct is that it is a statement of a companion (mawqūf)[1]: "The punishment for the sorcerers/magicians is that he should be stuck with a sword (executed)." In *Ṣaḥiḥ Al-Bukhārī*, Bajālah b. `Abadah narrated: "Umar b. Al-Khattab (رَضِيَ اللَّهُ عَنْهُ) wrote: 'Execute every sorcerer or sorceress.'" So Bajālah continued: "We executed three sorcerers."[2] Ḥafṣah (رَضِيَ اللَّهُ عَنْهَا) ordered an execution of a slave woman who practiced magic on her, so she was executed.[3] The same has been reported from Jundub (رَضِيَ اللَّهُ عَنْهُ).[4] Aḥmad said: "Execution of sorcerers (magicians) is attested by three Companions of the Prophet (صَلَّى اللَّهُ عَلَيْهِ وَسَلَّمَ).[5]

---

1 — That which is correct is that it is a statement of the companion (رَضِيَ اللَّهُ عَنْهُ). The chain leading up to the Messenger (صَلَّى اللَّهُ عَلَيْهِ وَسَلَّمَ) is weak as it has a narrator called Ismā'īl b. Muslim in it. Ismā'īl has been deemed weak by at-Tirmidhī, al-Bukhārī in (*Aḍ-Ḍu'afā Aṣ-Ṣaghīr*: no.19) and Sh.Al-Albānī in (*Aḍ-Ḍa'īfah*: 1446), who also declared the ascription to the Messenger (صَلَّى اللَّهُ عَلَيْهِ وَسَلَّمَ) as weak. So therefore, it is mawqūf. See (*Aḍ-Ḍa'īfah*: 1446)

2 — This actual wording is in: *Al-Musnad* (3/196), *Sunan Abī Dāwūd* (3043) and others. Authenticated by Ibn Ḥazm in *al-Maḥallā*: (12/414) and others.

3 — *Muṣannaf ibn Abī Shaybah*: (29583,28491) and *Muṣannaf 'Abir-Razzāq*: (18748). Ḥanbal b. Isḥāq stated that his uncle (al-Imām Aḥmad) said that the ruler is the one who judges regarding the sorcerer's execution. The decision and ruling lie with him. See *al-Jāmi'* of al-Khallāl: (1/530).

4 — *Muṣannaf 'Abir-Razzāq*: (18748)

5 — *Al-Jāmi'* of al-Khallāl: (1/529 no.1345).

ISSUES OF THIS CHAPTER:

1. The explanation of the verse in Al-Baqarah (2:102).
2. The explanation of the verse in An-Nisā(4:51).
3. The meaning of Al-Jibt and At-Ṭāghūt and the difference between the two.
4. At- Ṭāghūt could be among jinns or humans.
5. Details of seven deadly sins which are strictly forbidden.
6. Sorcerers or magicians are disbelievers (Kafir).
7. [The position] that the sorcerers/magicians should be executed and no repentance is accepted.
8. Sorcerers were found among the Muslims during the period of 'Umar (رَضِيَ اللَّهُ عَنْهُ). So how about thereafter?

CHAPTER EXERCISES

1. What is the definition of siḥr (magic)?
2. Name the seven destroyers mentioned in the ḥadīth of Abī Hurayrah (رَضِيَ اللَّهُ عَنْهُ).
3. Why do some scholars hold that the magician intended in this chapter takes the ruling of a disbeliever?
4. What is the relevance of mentioning Magic in this book?
5. Who is legislated to execute the punishment for magic?

CHAPTER EXERCISES

CHAPTER EXERCISES

CHAPTER EXERCISES

CHAPTER 24:

Clarification on Some Types of Magic

قَالَ أَحْمَدُ: حَدَّثَنَا مُحَمَّدُ بْنُ جَعْفَرٍ، حَدَّثَنَا عَوْفٌ، عَنْ حَيَّانُ بْنُ الْعَلَاءِ، حَدَّثَنَا قَطَنُ بْنُ قَبِيصَةَ، عَنْ أَبِيهِ، أَنَّهُ سَمِعَ النَّبِيَّ صَلَّى ٱللَّهُ عَلَيْهِ وَسَلَّمَ قَالَ: «إِنَّ الْعِيَافَةَ، وَالطَّرْقَ، وَالطِّيَرَةَ؛ مِنَ الْجِبْتِ». قَالَ عَوْفٌ: «الْعِيَافَةُ: زَجْرُ الطَّيْرِ، وَالطَّرْقُ: الْخَطُّ يُخَطُّ بِالأَرْضِ». وَالْجِبْتُ - قَالَ الْحَسَنُ-: «رَنَّةُ الشَّيْطَانِ». إِسْنَادُهُ جَيِّدٌ، وَلِأَبِي دَاوُدَ وَالنَّسَائِيِّ وَابْنِ حِبَّانَ فِي صَحِيحِهِ الْمُسْنَدُ مِنْهُ.

Aḥmad reported: Muḥammad b. Ja'far narrated from 'Auf, who narrated from Ḥayyān b. Al- `Alā',[1] from Qaṭan b. Qabiṣah, from his father (رَضِيَ ٱللَّهُ عَنْهُ), that he heard the Prophet (صَلَّى ٱللَّهُ عَلَيْهِ وَسَلَّمَ) say: "Verily, *al-'Iyāfah* (augury; birds flying to foretell events) and *aṭ-Ṭarq* (geomancy; drawing lines on earth to predict events) and *at-Ṭiyarah* (seeing bad omens) are *Al-Jibt* (magic)."[2] 'Auf said, "Al-'Iyāfah is letting a bird's flight foretell events, while aṭ-Ṭarq is drawing lines on the ground."[3]

Ḥasan said, "Al-Jibt is the scream of Shayṭān (devil)," with a chain of narrators that has been declared good. The ḥadīth was collected by Abū Dāwūd, An-Nasāī, and Ibn Ḥibbān that which is musnad from the above. [4]

1 — All of the narrators mentioned by the author are trustworthy (thiqqāt) except that there is conflict regarding Ḥayyān b. Al- `Alā' and his name. The correct stance is that his name is Ḥayyān b. 'Umayr Abū al-'Alā' (*Tahdhīb at-Tahdhīb*: 3/68) (*Al-Jarḥ wa at-Ta'dīl*: (1102). In addition, his pedigree as a narrator is of a lesser degree, he is acceptable (maqbūl)

2 — *Al-Musnad*: (25/256), *Sunan Abī Dāwūd*: (3907), *Muṣannaf ibn Abī Shaybah*: (26931), *Muṣannaf 'Abdur-Razzāq*: (19502), An-Nasā'ī in *Al-Kubrā*: (11043), *Ṣaḥiḥ ibn Ḥibbān*: (6131). Ibn Taymiyyah has classified this narration as ḥasan [sound, acceptable] in *Majmū al-Fatāwā*: (35/197). This is due to the presence of Ḥayyān.

3 — Al-'Iyāfah is also using the names, movement and sounds of birds to foretell events and determine optimism or pessimism. (Ibn Athīr, *An-Nihāyah*: 3/330). This narration is found, as previously mentioned, in *Al-Musnad* (25/256 no. 15915).

4 — The author intends here that these books of ḥadīth he has highlighted only contain the statement of the Messenger (صَلَّى ٱللَّهُ عَلَيْهِ وَسَلَّمَ) in this section. However, in *Sunan Abī Dāwūd*: (3907), the statement of 'Auf is mentioned albeit separately.

وَعَنِ ابْنِ عَبَّاسٍ رَضِيَ اللَّهُ عَنْهُمَا قَالَ: قَالَ رَسُولُ اللهِ صَلَّى اللَّهُ عَلَيْهِ وَسَلَّمَ: «مَنِ اقْتَبَسَ شُعْبَةً مِنَ النُّجُومِ فَقَدِ اقْتَبَسَ شُعْبَةً مِنَ السِّحْرِ؛ زَادَ مَا زَادَ».. رَوَاهُ أَبُو دَاوُدَ، بِإِسْنَادٍ صَحِيحٍ.

Abū Dāwūd reported in his book with an authentic chain that Ibn 'Abbās (رَضِيَ اللَّهُ عَنْهُمَا) narrated that Allāh's Messenger (صَلَّى اللَّهُ عَلَيْهِ وَسَلَّمَ) said: "Whoever acquires a branch of knowledge from the stars, has learned a part of sorcery (magic). The more an individual learns from it, the greater the sin."[1]

1 — *Al-Musnad*: (3/403), Abū Dāwūd (3905), Ibn Mājah: (3726) and others. Shaykh al-Islām ibn Taymiyyah: (*Majmū al Fatāwā* 35/193), Sh. al-Albānī: (*aṣ-Ṣaḥīḥah*: 793) and others, also authenticated this chain.

وَلِلنَّسَائِيِّ مِنْ حَدِيثِ أَبِي هُرَيْرَةَ رَضِيَ اللَّهُ عَنْهُ: «مَنْ عَقَدَ عُقْدَةً ثُمَّ نَفَثَ فِيهَا فَقَدْ سَحَرَ، وَمَنْ سَحَرَ فَقَدْ أَشْرَكَ، وَمَنْ تَعَلَّقَ شَيْئًا وُكِلَ إِلَيْهِ».

In An-Nasā'ī,[1] Abū Hurayrah (رَضِيَ اللَّهُ عَنْهُ) has reported that: "Whoever ties a knot and blows on it, has carried out sorcery, and whoever performs sorcery has committed Shirk. Whoever wears an amulet or talisman will be under its control."[2]

1 — *Al-Kubrā*: (3528) and *Aṣ-Ṣughrā*: (4079).

2 — There are two discrepancies in this ḥadīth. Firstly, in the chain, al-Ḥasan narrates from Abī Hurayrah; this is an area of contention between the scholars of ḥadīth. The majority hold that they never met, making the chain disconnected. Secondly, there is a narrator in this chain called 'Abbād b. Maysarh. Many scholars have deemed him weak like; Aḥmad, Yaḥyā b. Ma'īn and Abī Dāwūd (*Tahdhīb at-Tahdhīb*: 5/107-108), (*Mīzān al-I'tidāl*: 2/378 no. 4147). However, the last part of the narration; "Whoever wears an amulet or talisman will be under its control" is supported by the narration of 'Abdullāh b. Ukaīm (رَضِيَ اللَّهُ عَنْهُ) (*al-Musnad*: 18781, 18786), making this part alone acceptable (ḥasan). See *Ghāyatul-Marām*: (1/175).

وَعَـنِ ابْـنِ مَسْـعُودٍ رَضِيَ اللَّهُ عَنْهُ؛ أَنَّ رَسُـولَ اللـهِ صَلَّى اللَّهُ عَلَيْهِ وَسَلَّمَ قَـالَ: «أَلَا هَـلْ أُنَبِّئُكُـمْ مَـا الْعَضْـهُ؟ هِـيَ النَّمِيمَـةُ؛ الْقَالَـةُ بَيْـنَ النَّاسِ». رَوَاهُ مُسْلِمٌ. وَلَهُمَـا عَـنِ ابْنِ عُمَـرَ رَضِيَ اللَّهُ عَنْهُ؛ أَنَّ رَسُـولَ اللهِ صَلَّى اللَّهُ عَلَيْهِ وَسَلَّمَ قَـالَ: «إِنَّ مِـنَ الْبَيَـانِ لَسِـحْرًا».

Ibn Mas'ūd (رَضِيَ اللَّهُ عَنْهُ) reported that Allāh's Messenger (صَلَّى اللَّهُ عَلَيْهِ وَسَلَّمَ) said: "Shall I not tell you what Al-'Aḍh (literally: lying, sorcery, etc.) is? It is conveying false rumors to cause disputes between people." [Reported by Muslim][1] Both *Sahih* collectors reported from Ibn 'Umar (رَضِيَ اللَّهُ عَنْهُمَا) that Allāh's Messenger (صَلَّى اللَّهُ عَلَيْهِ وَسَلَّمَ) said "Some eloquence can tantamount to sorcery."[2]

1 — Muslim: (2606)

2 — Al-Bukhārī: (5146) From the narration of 'Abdullāh b. 'Umar (رَضِيَ اللَّهُ عَنْهُمَا) as referenced by the author. As for the reference to *Ṣaḥīḥ Muslim*: (869), then this was narrated by 'Ammār b.Yāsir (رَضِيَ اللَّهُ عَنْهُ).

ISSUES OF THIS CHAPTER:

1. Al-'Iyāfah, at-Ṭarq, at-Ṭiyarah are three kinds of al-Jibt (sorcery/magic).
2. Al-'Iyāfah and At-Tarq are explained.
3. Astrology too is a kind of sorcery.
4. Tying knots and blowing over them is also sorcery.
5. An-Namimah (tale-carrying, backbiting) is also a form of sorcery.
6. Sometimes, talking superfluously and eloquently can too be sorcery.

CHAPTER EXERCISES

1. What is the connection between this chapter and the last?
2. What do the magician and the soothsayer have in common?
3. Why is this chapter mentioned in the Book of at-Tawḥīd?
4. What is Al-'Aḍh?
5. Why is tale carrying described as magic?

CHAPTER EXERCISES

CHAPTER EXERCISES

CHAPTER EXERCISES

Page 252

CHAPTER 25:

What Has Come Regarding Soothsayers and the Like

رَوَى مُسْلِمٌ فِي صَحِيحِهِ عَنْ بَعْضِ أَزْوَاجِ النَّبِيِّ صَلَّى اللَّهُ عَلَيْهِ وَسَلَّمَ، عَنِ النَّبِيِّ صَلَّى اللَّهُ عَلَيْهِ وَسَلَّمَ قَالَ: «مَنْ أَتَى عَرَّافًا فَسَأَلَهُ عَنْ شَيْءٍ فَصَدَّقَهُ؛ لَمْ تُقْبَلْ لَهُ صَلَاةٌ أَرْبَعِينَ يَوْمًا». وَعَنْ أَبِي هُرَيْرَةَ رَضِيَ اللَّهُ عَنْهُ، عَنِ النَّبِيِّ صَلَّى اللَّهُ عَلَيْهِ وَسَلَّمَ قَالَ: «مَنْ أَتَى كَاهِنًا فَصَدَّقَهُ بِمَا يَقُولُ؛ فَقَدْ كَفَرَ بِمَا أُنْزِلَ عَلَى مُحَمَّدٍ صَلَّى اللَّهُ عَلَيْهِ وَسَلَّمَ». رَوَاهُ أَبُو دَاوُدَ.

Muslim recorded in his *Ṣaḥiḥ*, from some of the wives of the Prophet (صَلَّى اللَّهُ عَلَيْهِ وَسَلَّمَ) that he said: "Whoever goes to a fortuneteller and asks him to foretell and believes in his words, his prayer is rejected for forty days."[1] Abū Hurayrah (رَضِيَ اللَّهُ عَنْهُ) narrated that the Prophet (صَلَّى اللَّهُ عَلَيْهِ وَسَلَّمَ) said: "Whoever visits a soothsayer and believed in his words, has disbelieved in that which was revealed to Muḥammad (صَلَّى اللَّهُ عَلَيْهِ وَسَلَّمَ)." (Abū Dāwūd)[2]

1 — *Muslim*: (2230) narrated by the Mother of the believers Ḥafṣah (رَضِيَ اللَّهُ عَنْهَا). His statement "*...believes in his words*" is not in *Ṣaḥīḥ Muslim* but rather it is in the *Musnad* of al-Imām Aḥmad: (27:197) with an authentic chain.

2 — *Al-Musnad*: (15/164), Abū Dāwūd: (3904), At-Tirmidhī: (135), An-Nasā'ī in *al-Kubrā*: (8967,8968), Ibn Mājah: (639) and others. Authenticated by Sh. Al-Albānī in *al-Irwā'*: (7/68-70) and Sh. Aḥmad Shākir in his checking of *al-Musnad*: (1/244). This narration is classified as ṣaḥiḥ.

وَلِلْأَرْبَعَةِ وَالْحَاكِمِ- وَقَالَ: صَحِيحٌ عَلَى شَرْطِهِمَا- عَنْ [ ] «مَنْ أَتَى عَرَّافًا أَوْ كَاهِنًا فَصَدَّقَهُ بِمَا يَقُولُ؛ فَقَدْ كَفَرَ بِمَا أُنْزِلَ عَلَى مُحَمَّدٍ ». وَلِأَبِي يَعْلَى بِسَنَدٍ جَيِّدٍ عَنِ ابْنِ مَسْعُودٍ مِثْلُهُ مَوْقُوفًا.

The other four *Sunan* and Al-Ḥakim also reported this Hadith (of Abū Hurairah رَضِيَ اللَّهُ عَنْهُ)[1] and classified it as ṣaḥiḥ (authentic): "Whoever visits a fortuneteller or a soothsayer and believes in his words, has disbelieved in what was revealed to Muḥammad (صَلَّى اللَّهُ عَلَيْهِ وَسَلَّمَ)."[2] Abū Ya'lā reported a similar Hadith with a good chain that stops at Ibn Mas'ūd (رَضِيَ اللَّهُ عَنْهُ), Mawqūf.[3]

---

1 — There is a blank space in a few of the manuscripts for this book. Sh. Sulayman (the grandson of the author mentions that it is the name of the narrator missing; Abū Hurayrah (رَضِيَ اللَّهُ عَنْهُ) who heard it from The Messenger (صَلَّى اللَّهُ عَلَيْهِ وَسَلَّمَ) (*At-Taysīr*: 349).

2 — The author (رَحِمَهُ اللَّهُ) mentions that this narration is found in the four books of *Sunan* which is not the case. it is actually reported in *al-Musnad*: (15/331), al-Bayhaqī: (8/135), al-Ḥākim: (1/8) who authenticated it with Ad-Dhahabī agreeing with him in *Al-Kabā'ir*: (72). Sh. Sulaymān Āli ash-Shaykh also authenticated the chain (isnad) stating its conditions are on the same level as al-Bukhārī and Muslim: (*At-Taysīr*: 349).

3 — Abū Ya'lā: (9/280 no. 5408) who correctly stated that the narrators are all trustworthy.

وَعَنْ عِمْرَانَ بْنِ حُصَيْنٍ رَضِيَ اللَّهُ عَنْهُ مَرْفُوعًا: «لَيْسَ مِنَّا مَنْ تَطَيَّرَ أَوْ تُطُيِّرَ لَهُ، أَوْ تَكَهَّنَ أَوْ تُكُهِّنَ لَهُ، أَوْ سَحَرَ أَوْ سُحِرَ لَهُ، وَمَنْ أَتَى كَاهِنًا فَصَدَّقَهُ بِمَا يَقُولُ؛ فَقَدْ كَفَرَ بِمَا أُنْزِلَ عَلَى مُحَمَّدٍ صَلَّى اللَّهُ عَلَيْهِ وَسَلَّمَ». رَوَاهُ الْبَزَّارُ بِإِسْنَادٍ جَيِّدٍ. وَرَوَاهُ الطَّبَرَانِيُّ فِي الأَوْسَطِ بِإِسْنَادٍ حَسَنٍ مِنْ حَدِيثِ ابْنِ عَبَّاسٍ رَضِيَ اللَّهُ عَنْهُمَا دُونَ قَوْلِهِ: «وَمَنْ أَتَى...» إلى آخره.

'Imrān bin Ḥuṣain (رَضِيَ اللَّهُ عَنْهُ) narrates in a Marfū` Hadith [that Allāh's Messenger (صَلَّى اللَّهُ عَلَيْهِ وَسَلَّمَ) said]: "He is not from us the one who seeks omens or has omens interpreted for him; or who practices fortunetelling or has his fortunes told for him [...] or who practices sorcery and magic or goes to have it done for him, and whoever goes to a fortuneteller and believes in what he says has disbelieved in that which was revealed to Muḥammad (صَلَّى اللَّهُ عَلَيْهِ وَسَلَّمَ)." [Reported by Al-Bazzār with a good chain of narrators].[1] The same was reported by Aṭ-Ṭabarānī in *Al-Awsat* with a fair chain of narrators from Ibn 'Abbās (رَضِيَ اللَّهُ عَنْهُمَا) bar the wording: "Whoever goes to... (until the end)".[2]

1 — Al-Bazzār: (3578). The narrators were also deemed trustworthy by Al-Haythamī in *al-Majma'*: (5/117). Sh. Al-Albānī classified this narration as authentic (ṣaḥiḥ) in *as-Ṣaḥiḥah*: (2195).

2 — Aṭ-Ṭabarānī in *al-Awsat*: (4/301 no.4262). In this chain is Zam'ah b. Ṣāliḥ who is a weak narrator: (*Al-Jarḥ wa at-Ta'dīl* of ibn Abī Ḥātim: 3/624 no 2823). However, the previous narration strengthens it to the level of ḥasan as mentioned by the author (رَحِمَهُ اللَّهُ).

قال الْبَغَـوِيُّ: «الْعَـرَّافُ: الَّـذِي يَدَّعِـي مَعْرِفَـةَ الأُمُـورِ بِمُقَدِّمَـاتٍ يَسْـتَدِلُّ بِهَـا عَلَـى الْمَسْـرُوقِ وَمَكَانِ الضَّالَّـةِ وَنَحْـوِ ذَلِـكَ». وَقِيـلَ: هُـوَ الْكَاهِـنُ، وَالْكَاهِـنُ هُـوَ الَّـذِي يُخْبِـرُ عَـنِ الْمُغَيَّبَـاتِ فِـي الْمُسْـتَقْبَلِ. وَقِيـلَ: الَّـذِي يُخْبِـرُ عَمَّـا فِـي الضَّمِيرِ. وَقَـالَ أَبُـو الْعَبَّـاسِ ابْـنُ تَيْمِيَّـةَ: «الْعَـرَّافُ: اسْـمٌ لِلْكَاهِـنِ وَالْمُنَجِّـمِ وَالرَّمَّـالِ وَنَحْوِهِـمْ مِمَّـنْ يَتَكَلَّـمُ فِـي مَعْرِفَـةِ الأُمُـورِ بِهَـذِهِ الطُّـرُقِ». وَقَـالَ ابْـنُ عَبَّـاسٍ - فِـي قَـوْمٍ يَكْتُبُـونَ ((أَبَـا جَـادٍ))، وَيَنْظُـرُونَ فِـي النُّجُـومِ-: «مَـا أَرَى مَـنْ فَعَـلَ ذَلِـكَ لَـهُ عِنْـدَ اللهِ مِـنْ خَلَاقٍ».

Imam Al-Baghawī, "*Al-'Arrāf* is a person who claims to foresee matters to identify stolen items and the place of lost things and the like." Some said, it is the *Kāhin*; and *Kāhin* is the one who foretells of unseen matters in the future. It is also said that it is the one who informs of the inner secrets."[1] Abul-Abbās (ibn Taymiyyah) said, "*Al-'Arrāf* is a name for the fortuneteller and the astrologer (*Al-Munajjim*), and the diviner (*Ar-Rammal*), and their likes who speak of having knowledge of (unseen) matters in similar ways."[2] Ibn Abbās (رَضِيَ اللَّهُ عَنْهُمَا) said about those people who write *Abā Jād* (alphabet; to use in soothsaying, fortunetelling — which is a talisman in reality) and gaze at the stars believing in their influences on the earth: "I do not see that whoever does such has any share (in paradise) with Allāh."[3]

1 — *Sharḥ as-Sunnah of al-Baghawī*: (12/182).

2 — *Majmū al-Fatāwā*: (35/173).

3 — *Muṣannaf ibn Abī Shaybah*: (26161), *Muṣannaf 'Abdir-Razzāq*: (19805) with a sound chain.

ISSUES OF THIS CHAPTER:

1. Belief in a soothsayer and faith in the Qur'ān cannot coexist.
2. The affirmation that to do so (i.e. believe in a Kahin) is disbelief.
3. The mentioning of the one whose fortune is told.
4. The mentioning of the one for whom an omen is sought.
5. The mentioning of the one for whom sorcery is done.
6. The mentioning of the one who learns Abjad (use of alphabet in soothsaying or astrology).
7. The difference between the Kahin and the 'Arraf.

CHAPTER EXERCISES

1. What is an ar-Arrāf?
2. What is the ruling on the one who visits a soothsayer?
3. What is the meaning of an omen? How does this oppose at-Tawhīd?
4. What is the ruling on the one who visits a soothsayer and believes him?
5. What is Abā Jād? What is its significance to this chapter?

CHAPTER EXERCISES

CHAPTER EXERCISES

CHAPTER 26:

Curing Magical Spells

عَنْ جَابِرٍ رَضِيَ اللَّهُ عَنْهُ؛ أَنَّ رَسُولَ اللهِ صَلَّى اللَّهُ عَلَيْهِ وَسَلَّمَ سُئِلَ عَنِ النُّشْرَةِ، فَقَالَ: «هِيَ مِنْ عَمَلِ الشَّيْطَانِ».
رَوَاهُ أَحْمَدُ - بِسَنَدٍ جَيِّدٍ - وَأَبُو دَاوُدَ، وَقَالَ: سُئِلَ أَحْمَدُ عَنْهَا؛ فَقَالَ: ابْنُ مَسْعُودٍ رَضِيَ اللَّهُ عَنْهُ يَكْرَهُ هَذَا كُلَّهُ

Jabir (رَضِيَ اللَّهُ عَنْهُ) narrates that Allāh's Messenger (صَلَّى اللَّهُ عَلَيْهِ وَسَلَّمَ) was asked about An-Nushrah (the act of seeking a cure from magical spells/incantation), he (صَلَّى اللَّهُ عَلَيْهِ وَسَلَّمَ) said, «It is one of the acts of ash-Shayṭān." [Aḥmad and Abū Dāwūd have reported it with a good chain of narrators (isnād)].[1] Abū Dāwūd reported that when asked by Aḥmad about this, he said: "Ibn Mas'ūd disliked all this."[2]

1 — *Al-Musnad*: (22/40), Abū Dāwūd: (3867). Ibn al-Mufliḥ in *al-Ādāb ash-Shar'iyyah* (3/63) that the chain is good. Sh.Al-Albāni classified this narration as authentic: (*Aṣ-Ṣaḥiḥah*: 2760).

2 — Ibn al-Mufliḥ mentioned this in *al-Ādāb as-Shar'iyyah*: 3/63)

وَفِي الْبُخَارِيِّ عَنْ قَتَادَةَ: قُلْتُ لِابْنِ الْمُسَيَّبِ: رَجُلٌ بِهِ طِبٌّ أَوْ يُؤَخَّذُ عَنِ امْرَأَتِهِ؛ أَيُحَلُّ عَنْهُ أَوْ يُنَشَّرُ؟ قَالَ: «لَا بَأْسَ بِهِ، إِنَّمَا يُرِيدُونَ بِهِ الإِصْلَاحَ، فَأَمَّا مَا يَنْفَعُ فَلَمْ يُنْهَ عَنْهُ». انْتَهَى

Al-Bukhārī reports from Qatādah: I said to Ibn Al-Musayyab, "A man is under a magical spell or is unable to cohabitate with his wife, should we treat him by An-Nushrah or apply some other means to cure the spell/sorcery?' Ibn Al-Musayyab replied, "It is alright because they intend restoration or mending. That which benefits is not forbidden."[1] End of quote.

1 — Al-Bukhārī mentioned it in a suspended chain (Mu'allaq). It was connected in *Muṣannaf ibn Abī Shaybah*: (239890), Ibn 'Abdil-Barr: (*At-Tamhīd*: 6/244) and Ibn Ḥajr in *at-Taghlīq*: (5/49) who declared the chain as authentic.

وَرُوِيَ عَنِ الْحَسَنِ أَنَّهُ قَالَ: «لَا يَحُلُّ السِّحْرَ إِلَّا سَاحِرٌ».

It has been ascribed to Al-Ḥasan that he said: "Only a sorcerer (magician) can break the spell of another sorcerer."[1]

1 — In *At-Taghlīq*: (5/49) and *al-Fatḥ*: (20/244) Ibn Ḥajr mentions this quote and authenticated its chains.

قَالَ ابْنُ الْقَيِّمِ: «النُّشْرَةُ: حَلُّ السِّحْرِ عَنِ الْمَسْحُورِ، وَهِيَ نَوْعَانِ: أَحَدُهُمَا: حَلٌّ بِسِحْرٍ مِثْلِهِ، وَهُوَ الَّذِي مِنْ عَمَلِ الشَّيْطَانِ، وَعَلَيْهِ يُحْمَلُ قَوْلُ الْحَسَنِ، فَيَتَقَرَّبُ النَّاشِرُ وَالْمُنْتَشِرُ إِلَى الشَّيْطَانِ بِمَا يُحِبُّ، فَيُبْطِلُ عَمَلَهُ عَنِ الْمَسْحُورِ. وَالثَّانِي: النُّشْرَةُ بِالرُّقْيَةِ، وَالتَّعَوُّذَاتِ، وَالدَّعَوَاتِ، وَالأَدْوِيَةِ الْمُبَاحَةِ؛ فَهَذَا جَائِزٌ».

Ibn Al-Qayyim said: "An-Nushrah is removing the effects of sorcery from the affected one, and it is of two types:

1) The use of magic (sorcery) to remove the effects of another magic and it is an act of Shayṭān to which the comment of Imam Al-Hasan applies i.e.,that the one who performs sorcery and the patient, both get closer to Shayṭān by that which he loves. Shayṭān then removes the effects of magic from the afflicted.

2) The effects of magic can be removed by making recitation of Qur'ānic verses (Ruqyah); by offering legitimate supplications as well as by using permissible medical treatment. This type of Nushrah is permissible."[1]

1 — *I'lām al-Muwaqq'īn*: (4/397)

ISSUES OF THIS CHAPTER:

1. Prohibition of An-Nushrah.
2. The difference between the prohibited and permitted ways to remove such problems.

CHAPTER EXERCISES

1. What is an-Nushrah?
2. What is the relevance of this chapter to At-Tawhīd?
3. What is the position of 'Abdullāh b. Mas'ūd regarding An-Nushrah?
4. What is the position of Ibn al-Qayyim regarding An-Nushrah?
5. What are the correct ways to cure someone afflicted with magic?

CHAPTER EXERCISES

CHAPTER EXERCISES

CHAPTER 27:

What is Mentioned Regarding Belief in Omens

وَقَوْلِ اللهِ تَعَالَى: ﴿أَلَا إِنَّمَا طَائِرُهُمْ عِندَ اللَّهِ وَلَٰكِنَّ أَكْثَرَهُمْ لَا يَعْلَمُونَ﴾ الأعراف: ١٣١

وَقَوْلُهُ: ﴿قَالُوا طَائِرُكُم مَّعَكُمْ﴾ يس: ١٩

Allāh the Most Exalted said: "Verily, their omens are with Allāh but most of them do not know." [7:131]

Allāh the Most Exalted said: "They said, 'Your omen is with yourselves!'" [36:19]

> وَعَـنْ أَبِـي هُرَيْـرَةَ رَضِيَ اللَّهُ عَنْهُ؛ أَنَّ رَسُـولَ اللـهِ صَلَّى اللَّهُ عَلَيْهِ وَسَلَّمَ قَـالَ: «لَا عَـدْوَى، وَلَا طِيَـرَةَ، وَلَا هَامَـةَ، وَلَا صَفَـرَ». أَخْرَجَـاهُ. زَادَ مُسْـلِمٌ: «وَلَا نَـوْءَ، وَلَا غُـولَ».
>
> Abū Hurayrah (رضي الله عنه) narrated that Allāh's Messenger (صلى الله عليه وسلم) said: "There is no 'Adwa (contagion or contagion of disease without Allāh's Permission), nor is there At-Ṭiyarah (any bad omen from birds), nor is there any Hāmah (the omen of the night bird/owl), nor is there (any bad omen in the month of) Ṣafar.[1] In Muslim's *Ṣaḥīḥ* he added: "...and no Naw' (constellation) and no Ghūl (ghost etc.)[2]

---

1 — Al-Bukhārī: (5707), Muslim: (1744)

2 — The portion *"no Naw'"* is from Abī Hurayrah (رضي الله عنه) in Muslim: (2220) and the porton *"no Ghūl"* is from the narration of Jābir (رضي الله عنه) which is also in Muslim: (2222, 107).

وَلَهُمَا عَنْ أَنَسٍ رَضِيَ اللَّهُ عَنْهُ قَالَ: قَالَ رَسُولُ اللهِ صَلَّى اللَّهُ عَلَيْهِ وَسَلَّمَ: «لَا عَدْوَى، وَلَا طِيَرَةَ، وَيُعْجِبُنِي الْفَأْلُ» قَالُوا: وَمَا الْفَأْلُ؟ قَالَ: «الْكَلِمَةُ الطَّيِّبَةُ».

Al-Bukhārī and Muslim reported from Anas (رَضِيَ اللَّهُ عَنْهُ) that the Prophet (صَلَّى اللَّهُ عَلَيْهِ وَسَلَّمَ) said: "No Adwā (contagion) and no Ṭiyarah (bad omen) but Al-Fa'l pleases me." They asked, "What is Al-Fa'l?" He (صَلَّى اللَّهُ عَلَيْهِ وَسَلَّمَ) answered, "It is the good word."[1]

1 — Al-Bukhārī: (5776), Muslim: (2224)

وَلِأَبِي دَاوُدَ بِسَنَدٍ صَحِيحٍ عَنْ عُقْبَةَ بْنِ عَامِرٍ رَضِيَ اللَّهُ عَنْهُ قَالَ: ذُكِرَتِ الطِّيَرَةُ عِنْدَ رَسُولِ اللهِ صَلَّى اللَّهُ عَلَيْهِ وَسَلَّمَ، فَقَالَ: «أَحْسَنُهَا: الْفَأْلُ، وَلَا تَرُدُّ مُسْلِمًا، فَإِذَا رَأَى أَحَدُكُمْ مَا يَكْرَهُ؛ فَلْيَقُلْ: اللَّهُمَّ لَا يَأْتِي بِالْحَسَنَاتِ إِلَّا أَنْتَ، وَلَا يَدْفَعُ السَّيِّئَاتِ إِلَّا أَنْتَ، وَلَا حَوْلَ وَلَا قُوَّةَ إِلَّا بِكَ».

In a sound Isnād, Abū Dāwūd reported that Uqbah b. Āmir (رَضِيَ اللَّهُ عَنْهُ) said: At-Ṭiyarah (taking bad omens) was once mentioned to Allāh's Messenger (صَلَّى اللَّهُ عَلَيْهِ وَسَلَّمَ) and he (صَلَّى اللَّهُ عَلَيْهِ وَسَلَّمَ) said, "The best form of it is Al-Fa'l (optimism or the expectation that an event will occur by Allāh's Permission). It does not repel a Muslim. Whenever any of you sees something he dislikes, he should say: *'O Lord, none brings about good except you! Only you prevent evil things! There is no power and no strength except with You.'*"[1]

---

1 — In the text of this book 'Uqbah b. Āmir (رَضِيَ اللَّهُ عَنْهُ) is mentioned as the narrator. However, it is in fact 'Arwa b. Āmir as is mentioned in *Abū Dāwūd*: (3919), *Al-Bayhaqī*: (8/139), *Muṣannaf Ibn Abī Shaybah*: (26920,30157) and others. In addition, this ḥadīth has two issues; 1) The actual narrator 'Arwa b. Āmir, there was doubt has as to whether he met the Messenger (صَلَّى اللَّهُ عَلَيْهِ وَسَلَّمَ) or not. 2) One of the narrators, Ḥabīb b. Abī Thābit is a mudallis (known to camouflage who he narrated from) [*Ṭabaqāt Al-Mudallisīn*: no. 69]. Due to this obscurity, in order to accept his narrations, he must use clear modes of transmission which he has not done here. For these reasons, this narration has been declared weak. See *Aḍ-Ḍa'īfah*: (1619) of Sh. Al-Albānī (رَحِمَهُ اللَّهُ).

وَعَنِ ابْنِ مَسْعُودٍ رَضِيَ اللَّهُ عَنْهُ مَرْفُوعًا: «الطِّيَرَةُ شِرْكٌ، الطِّيَرَةُ شِرْكٌ، وَمَا مِنَّا إِلَّا؛ وَلَكِنَّ اللهَ يُذْهِبُهُ بِالتَّوَكُّلِ».
رَوَاهُ أَبُو دَاوُدَ وَالتِّرْمِذِيُّ وَصَحَّحَهُ، وَجَعَلَ آخِرَهُ مِنْ قَوْلِ ابْنِ مَسْعُودٍ رَضِيَ اللَّهُ عَنْهُ.

It is narrated from Ibn Mas'ūd (رَضِيَ اللَّهُ عَنْهُ) in a marfū' hadith: "At-Ṭiyarah is Shirk, At-Ṭiyarah is Shirk. There is none among us who does not feel something in his heart about At-Ṭiyarah. But Allāh, due to deep trust in Him, removes it."[1] [This ḥadīth was reported by At-Tirmidhī and Abu Dāwūd.] and it is stated that its last part is the statement of Ibn Mas'ūd (رَضِيَ اللَّهُ عَنْهُ).[2]

1 — Abū Dāwūd: (1614), At-Tirmidhī: (1614), *Al-Musnad*: (6/213), *Muṣannaf Ibn Abī Shaybah*: (26919), Aṭ-Ṭaḥāwī in *Sharḥ Mushkil Al-Āthār*: (no.827,828,1737,1748). Authenticated by Al-Imām At-Tirmidhī who declared this narration as *ḥasan-ṣaḥiḥ* and Sh. Al-Albānī who classified this ḥadīth as *ṣaḥiḥ* in *Aṣ-Ṣaḥīḥah*: (429).

2 — This is mentioned by Sulaymān b. Ḥarb (the teacher of Al-Bukhārī), At-Tirmidhī: (1614), *At-Targhīb* of Al-Mundhirī: (4/63), *Fatḥ al-Bārī* of Ibn Ḥajr: (10/224).

وَلِأَحْمَدَ مِنْ حَدِيثِ ابْنِ عَمْرٍو : «مَنْ رَدَّتْهُ الطِّيَرَةُ عَنْ حَاجَتِهِ؛ فَقَدْ أَشْرَكَ»، قَالُوا: فَمَا كَفَّارَةُ ذَلِكَ؟ قَالَ: «أَنْ يَقُولَ: اللَّهُمَّ لَا خَيْرَ إِلَّا خَيْرُكَ، وَلَا طَيْرَ إِلَّا طَيْرُكَ، وَلَا إِلَهَ غَيْرُكَ». وَلَهُ مِنْ حَدِيثِ الْفَضْلِ بْنِ الْعَبَّاسِ ☒: «إِنَّمَا الطِّيَرَةُ مَا أَمْضَاكَ أَوْ رَدَّكَ».

Aḥmad reported from Ibn 'Amr (رضي الله عنه) the following Hadith: "Whoever is turned back by At-Ṭiyarah (bad omens) has committed Shirk." They asked, "What is the atonement for such a sin?" He (صلى الله عليه وسلم) answered, "To say: 'O Lord, there is no good except the good which You bestow. There is no omen that except which You decree. And there is no true deity worthy of worship except You.'"[1] Aḥmad also reported that Faḍl b. Abbas (رضي الله عنه) said: "At-Ṭiyarah is that which causes you to carry something out or not to."[2]

1 — *Musnad:* (11/623), Aṭ-Ṭabarānī in *Al-Kabīr:* (14622), Al-Haythamī in *Al-Majma':* (5/105). In the chain of this narration is Ibn Lahi'ah. He has been deemed weak by some of the scholars of ḥadīth for the latter part of his life (رحمه الله). However, if his student's name is *"Abdullāh"* in a chain, then it is accepted. They all narrated from him before he became weak. Ad-Darquṭnī mentioned from those named *"Abdullah"* is ibn Wahab; 'Abdullāh b.Wahb. (*Aḍ-Ḍu'afā wa Al-Matrūkīn:* 333). This narration has been narrated by 'Abdullah b. Wahb from Ibn Lahi'ah, so it is an authentic ḥadīth. (*Al-Jāmi' of 'Abdullāh b. Wahb:* no.656)

2 — *Musnad:* (3/327). This ḥadīth has some discrepancies;

- Muḥammad b.'Abdullāh b. 'Ulāthah is in the chain and has been criticized for making many errors (*At-Taqrīb* 6078).
- Maslamah al-Juhanī is in this chain (isnād). He is relatively unknown.

3) There is a disconnection between Maslamah al-Juhanī and the companion in this chain Faḍl (رضي الله عنه); they did not meet (*at-Taysīr* by Sh.Sulayman Āalī as-Shaykh: p.377). However, there are many narrations that support this ḥadīth: (*Al-Muṭālib al-Āliyah:* (11/186). The most one can say about this narration is that it is *ḥasan li ghairihi* (acceptable due to external support). Allāh knows best.

ISSUES OF THIS CHAPTER:

1. Reminding the meanings of the verses:

> "Verily, these evil omens are with Allāh but most of them know not"(7:31)

And..

> "Your evil omens be with you" (36: 19).

2. The negation of contagions.
3. The negation of any bad omen.
4. Repudiation of Hamah (Omen in the night-bird i.e. owl).
5. The negation of any bad omen in the month of Ṣafar.
6. Al-Fa'l (optimism) is not prohibited but it is desirable.
7. Explanation of al-Fa'l in detail.
8. There is no harm if such suspicion falls on the hearts while disliking it. Indeed, Allāh will keep safe the ones who trust in him
9. What should be said if such feelings occur.
10. The affirmation that At-Ṭiyarah is Shirk.
11. Explanation of the blameworthy and condemned At-Ṭiyarah.

CHAPTER EXERCISES

1. What is the link between this and the previous chapter?
2. Mention one example of belief in omens the author brings in this chapter.
3. Why is the belief in omens considered shirk?
4. What is the meaning of al-Fa'l (الفأل)?
5. Where did the belief in omens originate?

CHAPTER EXERCISES

CHAPTER EXERCISES

CHAPTER EXERCISES

CHAPTER 28:

What is said regarding Astrology (At-Tanjeem)

قَالَ الْبُخَارِيُّ فِي صَحِيحِهِ: «قَالَ قَتَادَةُ: خَلَقَ اللهُ هَذِهِ النُّجُومَ لِثَلَاثٍ: زِينَةً لِلسَّمَاءِ، وَرُجُومًا لِلشَّيَاطِينِ، وَعَلَامَاتٍ يُهْتَدَى بِهَا، فَمَنْ تَأَوَّلَ فِيهَا غَيْرَ ذَلِكَ أَخْطَأَ، وَأَضَاعَ نَصِيبَهُ، وَتَكَلَّفَ مَا لَا عِلْمَ لَهُ بِهِ». انْتَهَى

Al-Bukhari recorded in his *Ṣaḥīḥ* that Qatādah said: "Allāh created the stars for three purposes: (1) As ornaments of the heavens; (2) As missiles against the devils; (3) As signposts for travelers. Whoever interprets it as other than that is mistaken. Such a person lost his portion (on the Day of Resurrection), and has taken upon himself that which is beyond his knowledge."[1] [End of Quote]

---

1 — Al-Bukhārī reported this quote in a suspended chain (Mu'allaq): (3/107). In Aṭ-Ṭabarī: (17/185) and *Tafsīr ibn Abī Ḥātim*: (16536) the chain is connected.

وَكَرِهَ قَتَادَةُ تَعَلُّمَ مَنَازِلِ الْقَمَرِ، وَلَمْ يُرَخِّصِ ابْنُ عُيَيْنَةَ فِيهِ. ذَكَرَهُ حَرْبٌ عَنْهُمَا. وَرَخَّصَ فِي تَعَلُّمِ الْمَنَازِلِ أَحْمَدُ وَإِسْحَاقُ.

Ḥarb has reported that learning lunar phases was permitted by Aḥmad and Isḥāq (Ar-Rāhawayh), discouraged by Qatādah and prohibited by (Sufyan) ibn 'Uyaynah.[1]

1 — Masā'il ibn Ḥarb: (1/595)

وَعَنْ أَبِي مُوسَى رَضِيَ اللَّهُ عَنْهُ قَالَ: قَالَ رَسُولُ اللهِ صَلَّى اللَّهُ عَلَيْهِ وَسَلَّمَ: «ثَلَاثَةٌ لَا يَدْخُلُونَ الْجَنَّةَ: مُدْمِنُ الْخَمْرِ، وَقَاطِعُ الرَّحِمِ، وَمُصَدِّقٌ بِالسِّحْرِ». رَوَاهُ أَحْمَدُ وَابْنُ حِبَّانَ فِي صَحِيحِهِ.

Abu Musa (رَضِيَ اللَّهُ عَنْهُ) is reported to have said that Allāh's Messenger (صَلَّى اللَّهُ عَلَيْهِ وَسَلَّمَ) said: "Three (types of people) will not enter Paradise: (1) The habitual wine (alcohol) drinker; (2) The believer in sorcery (and astrology is among it); (3) The one who severs blood relations." [collected by Aḥmad, and Ibn Ḥibbān has mentioned this Hadith in his *Ṣaḥiḥ*].[1]

1 — *Al-Musnad*: (32/338). Authenticated by Sh. Albānī in *Ṣaḥīḥ At-Targhīb At-Tarhīb*: (2539)

ISSUES OF THIS CHAPTER:

1. The wisdom of creating the stars.
2. The refutation of those who claim otherwise.
3. The mentioning of the difference of opinions regarding the study of the lunar phases.
4. The punishment promised for those who believed in any aspect of sorcery though knowing fully well that sorcery is falsehood.

CHAPTER EXERCISES

1. What is at-Tanjīm?

2. What is the link between magic and at-Tanjīm?

3. Who are the three that are threatened with not entering Jannah?

4. What is the wisdom behind the creation of the stars?

5. Mention one evidence from this chapter for the impermissibility of speaking without knowledge.

CHAPTER EXERCISES

Page 288

CHAPTER EXERCISES

CHAPTER EXERCISES

CHAPTER 29:

Seeking Rain through the Lunar Phases (Constellation)

> وَقَوْلِ اللهِ تَعَالَى: ﴿وَتَجْعَلُونَ رِزْقَكُمْ أَنَّكُمْ تُكَذِّبُونَ﴾ الواقعة: ٨٢
>
> Allāh the Most Exalted said: "And instead (of thanking Allāh) for the provision He gives you, on the contrary, you deny Him (by disbelief)!" [56:82]

وَعَنْ أَبِي مَالِكٍ الأَشْعَرِيِّ رَضِيَٱللَّهُعَنْهُ؛ أَنَّ رَسُولَ اللهِ صَلَّىٱللَّهُعَلَيْهِوَسَلَّمَ قَالَ: «أَرْبَعٌ فِي أُمَّتِي مِنْ أَمْرِ الْجَاهِلِيَّةِ لَا يَتْرُكُونَهُنَّ: الْفَخْرُ بِالأَحْسَابِ، وَالطَّعْنُ فِي الأَنْسَابِ، وَالِاسْتِسْقَاءُ بِالنُّجُومِ، وَالنِّيَاحَةُ»، وَقَالَ: «النَّائِحَةُ إِذَا لَمْ تَتُبْ قَبْلَ مَوْتِهَا؛ تُقَامُ يَوْمَ الْقِيَامَةِ وَعَلَيْهَا سِرْبَالٌ مِنْ قَطِرَانٍ، وَدِرْعٌ مِنْ جَرَبٍ». رَوَاهُ مُسْلِمٌ.

Abū Mālik Al-Ash'arī (رَضِيَٱللَّهُعَنْهُ) narrated Allāh's Messenger (صَلَّىٱللَّهُعَلَيْهِوَسَلَّمَ) as saying: "My Ummah will not abandon four undesirable matters from the Period of Ignorance (period previous to Islam). They are:

- Haughtiness in ancestors;
- Defaming or slandering someone's lineage;
- Seeking rain through the stars, and
- Lamentation and wailing of women for the dead."

He (صَلَّىٱللَّهُعَلَيْهِوَسَلَّمَ) said, "If the bewailing woman does not repent before her death, she will be raised on the Day of the Resurrection covered with a dress of liquid pitch, and a cloak of itches." (Reported by Muslim)[1]

1 — Muslim: (934)

وَلَهُمَا عَنْ زَيْدِ بْنِ خَالِدٍ رَضِيَ اللَّهُ عَنْهُ قَالَ: صَلَّى لَنَا رَسُولُ اللهِ صَلَّى اللَّهُ عَلَيْهِ وَسَلَّمَ صَلَاةَ الصُّبْحِ بِالْحُدَيْبِيَةِ، عَلَى إِثْرِ سَمَاءٍ كَانَتْ مِنَ اللَّيْلِ، فَلَمَّا انْصَرَفَ أَقْبَلَ عَلَى النَّاسِ، فَقَالَ: «هَلْ تَدْرُونَ مَاذَا قَالَ رَبُّكُمْ؟» قَالُوا: اللهُ وَرَسُولُهُ أَعْلَمُ، قَالَ: «أَصْبَحَ مِنْ عِبَادِي مُؤْمِنٌ بِي وَكَافِرٌ، فَأَمَّا مَنْ قَالَ: مُطِرْنَا بِفَضْلِ اللهِ وَرَحْمَتِهِ؛ فَذَلِكَ مُؤْمِنٌ بِي كَافِرٌ بِالْكَوْكَبِ، وَأَمَّا مَنْ قَالَ: مُطِرْنَا بِنَوْءِ كَذَا وَكَذَا؛ فَذَلِكَ كَافِرٌ بِي مُؤْمِنٌ بِالْكَوْكَبِ».

In the two *Ṣaḥīḥ* collections Zayd b. Khalid (رَضِيَ اللَّهُ عَنْهُ) said: Allāh's Messenger (صَلَّى اللَّهُ عَلَيْهِ وَسَلَّمَ) led us in the Fajr prayer at Ḥudaibiyyah after a rainy night. After completing the prayer, he (صَلَّى اللَّهُ عَلَيْهِ وَسَلَّمَ) faced the people and said, "Do you know what your Lord has said?" The people replied, "Allāh and His Messenger know better." He said, "Allāh has said, '*In this morning, some of My slaves remained true believers and some became disbelievers; whoever said that the rain was due to the favors and mercy of Allāh, is the one who believes in Me and he disbelieves in the star, and whoever said that it rained because of a particular star, is a disbeliever in Me and a believer in the star.*'"[1]

1 — Al-Bukhārī: (846), Muslim: (71)

ولَهُمَا مِنْ حَدِيثِ ابْنِ عَبَّاسٍ مَعْنَاهُ، وَفِيهِ: قَالَ بَعْضُهُمْ: لَقَدْ صَدَقَ نَوْءُ كَذَا وَكَذَا؛ فَأَنْزَلَ اللهُ هَذِهِ الآيَاتِ: ﴿فَلَا أُقْسِمُ بِمَوَاقِعِ النُّجُومِ﴾ الواقعة: ٧٥ إِلَى قَوْلِهِ ﴿تُكَذِّبُونَ﴾ الواقعة: ٨٢

Al-Bukhārī and Muslim[1] also have reported a similar ḥadīth from Ibn 'Abbās (رَضِيَ اللَّهُ عَنْهُمَا) where it has been said that when some said that it rained because of such and such star. Then Allāh revealed the following verses: "So, I swear by the setting of the stars..." until His statement: "...you deny." [56:75-82]

1 — This narration is only found in Muslim: (73)

ISSUES OF THIS CHAPTER:

1. Explanation of the verses in Al-Wāqi 'ah (56: 75-82).
2. The four undesirable customs of the pre-Islamic period.
3. The acts of disbelief contained in some of them.
4. That some acts of disbelief do not expel one from the religion (of Islam).
5. The Statement of Allāh:

> "In this morning, some of (my slaves) remained as true believers and some became disbelievers..."

due to the favor bestowed upon them (of rain).

6. The understanding of Īmān in such a circumstance.
7. The understanding of Kufr (disbelief) in such a circumstance.
8. The understanding of his statement in response to some who verified: "It rained because of such and such star."
9. The scholar extracting understanding of this affair from his students by way of questioning to explain the issue as the Prophet (صَلَّى ٱللَّهُ عَلَيْهِ وَسَلَّمَ) said: "Do you know what your Lord has said (revealed)?"
10. The threat of punishment promised to the bewailing women.

CHAPTER EXERCISES

1. Name four traits of the days of ignorance mentioned in this chapter.
2. Why does Allāh swear by some of His creation?
3. Why is it impermissible for us to swear by the creation?
4. Where in this chapter do you find a refutation against those from the people of innovation who negate the attribute of speech for Allāh?
5. What is the legislated way of seeking rain?

CHAPTER EXERCISES

CHAPTER EXERCISES

CHAPTER EXERCISES

APPENDIX 1:

Answer Key for Chapter Questions (Chapters 1-29)

Introduction

1. The Jinn and Humankind have been created to worship Allāh alone without any partners. The proof of this is found in (Sūrah 51: Verse 56).

2. From the wisdom in the sending of the messengers is to call the people to worship Allāh alone. The proof of this is found in (Sūrah 16: Verse 36).

3. The rights of Allah upon His servants is an obligation. The rights of the servants upon Allah is a favor.

4. Allah mentioned dutifulness to one's parents after at-Tawḥīd in the same verse to show the importance of the issue.

5. The narration of Mu'ādh (رَضِيَ اللَّهُ عَنْهُ) gives us an example of the humility of the Messenger (صَلَّى اللَّهُ عَلَيْهِ وَسَلَّمَ). This is exemplified in his sharing the riding beast with his companion.

Chapter 1

1. This shows that Īsā (صَلَّى اللَّهُ عَلَيْهِ وَسَلَّمَ) is a worshiper of Allah and a caller to Tawḥīd. This is a refutation against both the Christians (as he is worshiper not to be worshiped) and the Jews (as he is Messenger of Allah).

2. The one that establishes and implements at-Tawḥīd and its prerequisites will be saved from the Hellfire. The person of at-Tawḥīd has been promised forgiveness from Allah. The person who dies upon at-Tawḥīd will enter Paradise.

3. It means that there is none has the right to be worshiped in truth except Allāh the Lord of the creation who has perfect names and attributes befitting to His majesty.

4. This necessitates that he is a worshiper and a messenger to be followed (صَلَّى اللَّهُ عَلَيْهِ وَسَلَّمَ).

5. It shows the virtue of at-Tawḥīd of worship and that which it necessitates from belief.

Chapter 2

1. Ibrahīm was a good example to be followed, devoutly obedient to Allah and a person of at-Tawḥīd who stayed fully away from polytheism.

2. The person who establishes at-Tawḥīd enters Paradise without being taken to account. Establishing at-Tawḥīd is the main characteristic of devout believers.

3. Ḥuṣain b. 'Abdur-Raḥmān made sure it was not assumed he was busy in worship when he was up at night but rather, he was stung.

4. Belief in omens contradicts at-Tawakkul (reliance on Allāh) and it contests with the Lordship of Allāh.

5. The virtues of the one who refrains from belief and reliance in omens and its likes and emphasizes the importance of reliance in Allāh the Creator of all things.

Chapter 3

1. The one who dies associating of partners with Allāh is devoid of Allāh's forgiveness.

2. The supplication of Ibrāhīm to Allāh is warning to all after him that they too should fear falling into shirk and refrain from complacency.

3. "....He forgives other than that to whom He pleases." [4:48, 116]. This proofs that Allah forgives other than major shirk and its likes.

4. The mentioning of the Hellfire in the ḥadīth of 'Abdullah b. Mas'ūd (رَضِيَ ٱللَّهُ عَنْهُ) is proof for an aspect for the hereafter, the Hellfire. In the ḥadīth of Jābir (رَضِيَ ٱللَّهُ عَنْهُ), we have a proof for the belief in Paradise.

5. The main categories of shirk are the minor and major shirk.

Chapter 4

1. The correct methodology in calling to Allāh is to begin with at-Tawḥīd, as is mentioned in the ḥadīth of the Messenger (صَلَّى ٱللَّهُ عَلَيْهِ وَسَلَّمَ) sending Mu'ādh (رَضِيَ ٱللَّهُ عَنْهُ) to Yemen. Likewise, this call has to be to Allāh and His Religion; the Qur'ān and Sunnah, and upon sure knowledge. This is shown in the statement of Allāh: '...This is my way; I call to Allāh with sure knowledge, I and whosoever follows me...' [12: 108].

2. The ḥadīth of Sahl b. Sa'd (رَضِيَ ٱللَّهُ عَنْهُ): "Where is 'Ali b. Abī Ṭālib?" They replied, "He is suffering from an eye ailment." He was sent for and brought. Allāh's Messenger (صَلَّى ٱللَّهُ عَلَيْهِ وَسَلَّمَ) then spat in his eyes and prayed for him, whereupon he was cured as if he did not have any ailments. This is proof of the prophethood of Muḥammad (صَلَّى ٱللَّهُ عَلَيْهِ وَسَلَّمَ).

3. From the virtues of calling to Allāh is that one being guided through you is better for you then the most valuable worldly commodity. This is from the ḥadīth of Sahl b. Sa'd (رَضِيَ اللَّهُ عَنْهُ).

4. From the benefits of the ḥadīth of Mu'ādh (رَضِيَ اللَّهُ عَنْهُ) are; the virtues of at-Tawḥīd, the virtues of the prescribed daily prayers, and the ill effects of

5. The importance of knowledge is mentioned in the statement of Allah: "I call to Allāh with sure knowledge." [12: 108]. Likewise, the status of knowledge can be shown in the sending of Mu'ādh (رَضِيَ اللَّهُ عَنْهُ). Mu'ādh was from the most knowledgeable of the companions showing that knowledge is imperative when calling to Allāh.

Chapter 5

1. The necessities of religion, life, and wealth are mentioned in the ḥadīth of Ṭāriq b. Ashyam (رَضِيَ اللَّهُ عَنْهُ).

2. Allāh said: "Those whom they call upon desire (for themselves) a means of getting close to their Lord (Allāh) [17:57]. This verse shows us that those who they call (worship) like the prophets, angels and the pious themselves worship Allāh and try to get close to Him. They need to worship Allāh so how can they be worshiped?!

3. The pillars of *lā ilāhā illā Allāh* are negation (of others deserved of worship) and affirmation (that worship is only for Allāh). This is shown in (Sūrah 43: Verses 28-27) and also in the ḥadīth of Ṭāriq b. Ashyam in *Ṣaḥīḥ Muslim*.

4. The explanation of at-Tawḥīd is shown in (Sūrah 43: Verses 28-27).

5. The pillars of worship are love, fear, and hope. Every act of worship must comprise of these three pillars. The proof of these pillars is found in (Sūrah 17: Verse 57). His statement "*...desire (for themselves) a means of getting close to their Lord (Allāh)...*" is proof for the pillar 'love'. "*Hoping for His Mercy*" is proof for the pillar 'hope'. "*Fearing His Torment*" is proof for the pillar 'fear'.

Chapter 6

1. Most of them do not believe in Allāh (His Lordship) except that they associate partners with Allāh (in worship). Belief in Allāh's Lordship is not sufficient.

2. Two examples where forbidding evil occurs when Ḥudhaifah (رَضِيَ اللَّهُ عَنْهُ) cut the twine worn by an individual and then read the verse: "Most of them do not believe in Allāh except that they still practice Shirk (polytheism)." [12:106].

3. Wearing objects to ward off evil adds to one's weakness as it compromising the strength of trusting in Allāh. It also breeds fear of the creation in the heart of the perpetrator.

4. Minor shirk is everything (statements and actions that leads to the major shirk that has itself been labeled as shirk in the Qur'ān and Sunnah. (See *Qawl as-Sadīd*: 32)

5. Major shirk takes one out of the fold of Islām. However, the one who falls into minor shirk is still a Muslim. Major shirk wipes out the good deeds of the perpetrator. As for minor shirk, this is not the case.

Chapter 7

1. In both this and the previous chapter are examples of shirk. This chapter is a continuation and completion of the previous one.

2. The affairs mentioned in this chapter require more detail and clarification as it relates to its ruling. As for the previous chapter, their ruling as shirk is clear and explicit. (See *I'ānah al-Mustafīd*: 1/199)

3. In the pre-Islamic era, the polytheist used to tie bowstrings on the necks of their camels to ward off the evil eye. This is the reason why the Messenger (صَلَّى ٱللَّهُ عَلَيْهِ وَسَلَّمَ) ordered the necklaces and bowstring be cut off from around the necks of camels.

4. The levels of forbidding the evil are of three levels; by one's arms if legislated, if not by one's speech, if not then at the very least, within one's heart.

5. When 'Abdullāh b. Mas'ūd saw with his wife a twine, this prompted him to relay the statement of the Messenger (صَلَّى ٱللَّهُ عَلَيْهِ وَسَلَّمَ) say: "Ar-Ruqā, At-Tamā'im, and At-Tiwalah are all acts of Shirk (polytheism)." (See *al-Mishkāt*: ḥadīth no.4552)

Chapter 8

1. In this chapter are further examples of acts of shirk.

2. Blessings are from Allāh hence it must be sought from Him.

3. The pagans derived 'al-Lāt' from Allāh, al-'Uzzā from al-'Azīz, and Manāt from al-Mannān. These were acts of shirk and denial of the lofty Names of Allāh.

4. The Messenger (صَلَّى ٱللَّهُ عَلَيْهِ وَسَلَّمَ) reprimanded his companions (رَضِيَ ٱللَّهُ عَنْهُمْ) even though they recently embraced Islām to show them the severity of shirk and the cautiousness one must have regarding it.

5. The for not following those before us from the Jews, Christians, and polytheist is his statement (صَلَّى ٱللَّهُ عَلَيْهِ وَسَلَّمَ) in a tone of rebuke: "You will surely follow the ways of those who came before you."

Chapter 9

1. The four affairs mentioned in this chapter that earn the cures of Allāh are; slaughtering for other than Allāh, cursing one's parents, sheltering a heretic, and altering the landmarks and boundaries of properties and land.

2. Slaughtering for other than Allāh, or fear of the creation or in other than Allāh's is shirk.

3. Slaughtering an animal to feed your guest is permissible as long as it is not done in the name of other than Allāh.

4. Slaughtering a sheep to fulfill your duty as a host is from generosity and good etiquette. As for slaughtering a sheep at a grave to get closer to its inhabitants, this is shirk.

5. In this chapter, the verse that shows the obligation of sincerity at all times is the statement of Allāh: "Say: Verily my prayer, my sacrifice, my living, and my dying are for Allāh, the Lord of all worlds. He has no partner. And of this, I have been commanded, and I am the first of the Muslims." [6:162,163]

Chapter 10

1. The previous chapter is fundamentally about the impermissibility of sacrificing for other than Allāh, which is shirk. As for this chapter, the main topic is the impermissibility of sacrificing for Allāh in a place where others have been sacrificed for, as this leads to shirk.

2. The masjid intended in the verse; "Never stand you therein." [9:108] is Masjid aḍ-Ḍirār.

3. The meaning of Jāhiliyah in the ḥadīth of Thābit (رَضِيَ ٱللَّهُ عَنْهُ) is the period before the sending of Muḥammad (صَلَّى ٱللَّهُ عَلَيْهِ وَسَلَّمَ) as a Messenger.

4. 'Eid is a recurring festival pertaining to time and place. That which is of time (العيد الزمني) is 'Eid al-Fiṭr and 'Eid al-Aḍḥā. That which is of place (العيد المكاني) is where the people gather for worship like 'Arafah, Muzdalifah, and Minā.

5. In this chapter, the preservation of at-Tawḥīd is emphasized by the prohibition of performing any type of worship in a place where other than Allāh is worshiped.

Chapter 11

1. The meaning of a 'vow' is when a servant compels an act of obedience upon himself (by speech) when it was not in its origin obligatory.

2. Examples of a vow of obedience are; vowing to pray in the Prophets Masjid and vowing to give such and such in charity. Even though the Messenger (صَلَّى ٱللَّهُ عَلَيْهِ وَسَلَّمَ) warned against taking a vow. Once made fulfilling it is now obligatory.

3. Making a vow is prohibited because it breeds stinginess and miserliness in worship.

4. Allāh commended those who fulfilled their vows in His statement: "They (are those who) fulfill (their) vows..." [76:7]. This is proof that it is indeed worship.

5. It is impermissible to fulfill a vow to disobey Allāh. The proof of this in the ḥadīth of 'Aishah (رَضِيَ ٱللَّهُ عَنْهَا): "whoever made a vow that he will disobey Allāh, he should not disobey Him."

Chapter 12

1. Seeking from the creation from that which is only south from Allāh is shirk.

2. The statement of the Messenger (صَلَّى ٱللَّهُ عَلَيْهِ وَسَلَّمَ): *'I seek refuge in Allāh's perfect words from the evil which He created'* is proof that the speech of Allāh is not created. This because we do not seek refuge from the creation. We are commanded to seek refuge in the Speech of Allāh which is proof that It is not created.

3. It is permissible to seek aid from the creation for things that are within the realms of their ability.

4. The ḥadīth of Khawlah bint Ḥakīm (رَضِيَ ٱللَّهُ عَنْهَا) is proof that seeking refuge is worship.

5. When one says this supplication with the attentiveness of the heart and mind, no harm shall befall them until they depart from that place. In it is the virtue of the speech of Allāh.

Chapter 13

1. Seeking deliverance from the creation in that which is beyond their ability is major shirk. For example, seeking deliverance from the dead and the absent.

2. Those who invoke the dead or the absent are most astray as the invoked will not and cannot hear their invocations. Another intellectual refutation against those who invoke other than Allāh is that those whom they invoke can neither benefit nor harm them.

3. Proof that the Messenger (صَلَّى ٱللَّهُ عَلَيْهِ وَسَلَّمَ) is not a deity is his statement: "Verily, no one should seek deliverance from me. Indeed, it is from Allāh deliverance is sought."

4. An example of the Messenger's protectiveness of at-Tawḥīd is his statement (صَلَّى ٱللَّهُ عَلَيْهِ وَسَلَّمَ): "Verily, no one should seek deliverance from me. Indeed, it is from Allāh deliverance is sought."

5. From the affirmation of tawḥīd of worship through the tawḥīd of lordship is His statement: "So seek your provisions from Allāh (Alone) and worship Him (Alone)." [29:17]

Chapter 14

1. At-Tawḥīd is emphasized in his (صَلَّى ٱللَّهُ عَلَيْهِ وَسَلَّمَ) statement: " I will not be of any help to you before Allāh."

2. The meaning of "curse" (اللعن) is to be devoid of the Mercy of Allāh.

3. The Messenger (صَلَّى ٱللَّهُ عَلَيْهِ وَسَلَّمَ) invoked Allāh against Safwan b. Umaiyah and Suhail b. 'Amr and Al-Ḥārith b. Hishām.

4. The Messenger of Allāh (صَلَّى ٱللَّهُ عَلَيْهِ وَسَلَّمَ) was harmed in Uḥud. If he was aware of the unseen, this would not have happened. Allāh commanded the Messenger (صَلَّى ٱللَّهُ عَلَيْهِ وَسَلَّمَ) to say: if I had the knowledge of the Ghaib (unseen), I should have secured for myself an abundance of wealth, and no evil should have touched me? [7:188]

5. A refutation against tribalism and fanaticism is found in the statement of the Messenger (صَلَّى ٱللَّهُ عَلَيْهِ وَسَلَّمَ): "O people of Quraish" — or words similar to that effect — "sell your souls. I will not be of any help to you before Allāh."

Chapter 15

1. Proof that the angels are servants of Allāh is shown in his statement (صَلَّى ٱللَّهُ عَلَيْهِ وَسَلَّمَ): "...When the Words of Allāh fall upon the inhabitants of heaven, they are taken by shock and fall in prostration. The first of them to raise his head is the angel Jibrāīl..."

2. In this chapter one of the virtues of Jibrīl is that he is entrusted with the revelation and all the angels asked him: "What did our Lord say?"

3. The speech of Allāh affirmed in this chapter when the angels asked: "What did our Lord say?" Likewise, when the Messenger (صَلَّى ٱللَّهُ عَلَيْهِ وَسَلَّمَ) said: "When Allāh gives some order in the heaven..." Giving an order is from His speech (تَبَارَكَ وَتَعَالَىٰ).

4. The attribute of want (الإرادة) is mentioned in the statement of the Messenger (صَلَّى ٱللَّهُ عَلَيْهِ وَسَلَّمَ): "When Allāh wishes to reveal something to man."

5. The relationship between them is that soothsayers get untrusted information from the shayāṭīn.

Chapter 16

1. The conditions for a valid intercession is that Allāh has to be pleased with the one interceded for, and He has given permission for it.

2. Every single text in this chapter can be used as proof that Allāh alone deserves to be worshiped. The dominion is His alone, intercession is by His permission alone. Likewise, His statement: "Say: Call upon those whom you assert (to be associate gods) besides Allāh, they do not even possess the weight of an atom (or a small ant), either in the heavens or on the earth..." [34:22,23].

3. An intellectual proof mentioned in this chapter that refutes those who call upon other than Allah is His statement: "Say: Call upon those whom you assert (to be associate gods) besides Allāh, they do not even possess the weight of an atom (or a small ant), either in the heavens or on the earth..." [34:22,23].

4. The intercession that is polytheistic is rejected and invalid.

5. A major virtue of sincerity and at-Tawḥīd is found in the ḥadīth where Abū Hurayrah (رَضِيَ ٱللَّهُ عَنْهُ) asked the Prophet (صَلَّى ٱللَّهُ عَلَيْهِ وَسَلَّمَ): "Who will be the happiest of people with your intercession?" He (صَلَّى ٱللَّهُ عَلَيْهِ وَسَلَّمَ) said, "Whoever said *La ilāhā illa Allāh* sincerely with pure intention from his heart."

Chapter 17

1. There are two general types of guidance: The guidance of the heart which is exclusively for Allāh (التوفيق), and the guidance of clarification and propagation (الإرشاد).

2. In this chapter, the story of the death of Abī Ṭālib, the uncle of the Prophet (صَلَّىٱللَّهُعَلَيۡهِوَسَلَّمَ) is an example of the ill effects of bad companionship: "The two of them said, 'Would you forsake the religion of 'Abdul Muṭṭalib?!'"

3. In the narration of the death of Abī Ṭālib, the narrator quoted the statement: "The final word of Abū Ṭālib was that he was upon the religion of 'Abdul-Muṭṭalib." The narrator spoke in the third person so as not to utter the speech of disbelief in the first person.

4. The connection between this chapter and at-Tawḥīd is that the One who guides whom he (alone) so ever wills is the One that deserves to be worshiped alone without any partners.

5. Two additional benefits we can take from the story of the death of Abī Ṭālib are; [1] The Messenger (صَلَّىٱللَّهُعَلَيۡهِوَسَلَّمَ) could not guide his uncle so how can any type of worship be directed to him (صَلَّىٱللَّهُعَلَيۡهِوَسَلَّمَ)? [2] This story shows the importance of at-Tawḥīd and that no deed is accepted without it.

Chapter 18

1. The names of the idols worshiped in the time of Nuḥ (صَلَّىٱللَّهُعَلَيۡهِوَسَلَّمَ) were Wadd, Suwā', Yaghūth, Ya'ūq, and Nasr.

2. In this chapter, the proof for closing the gates that lead to evil from the offset is in the commentary of Ibn 'Abbās (رَضِيَٱللَّهُعَنۡهُمَا): "...Satan inspired them to set up statues in their honor, placed in their gatherings. They gave these statues the names of those righteous people. At this point, they did not worship them until they passed away and knowledge of their origins were forgotten, the statues were then worshipped."

3. Exaggeration for the righteous coupled with ignorance were the reasons the first act of shirk occurred.

4. We can say from the story of Wadd, Suwā', Yaghūth, Ya'ūq, and Nasr that the initiation of their statues was an act of innovation inspired by Shayṭān. This ultimately led to shirk.

5. In this chapter, we find that in the story of Wadd, Suwā', Yaghūth, Ya'ūq, and Nasr once knowledge and its people had diminished, ignorance became widespread and so the people fell into shirk.

Chapter 19

1. The norm of those before from the Christian and Jews was to take the graves of their pious as places of worship.

2. Marfū' is a terminology used in the science of ḥadīth to signify that a statement, action, or acknowledgment has been ascribed to the Messenger (صَلَّى ٱللَّهُ عَلَيْهِ وَسَلَّمَ) directly or indirectly.

3. The analogy of the superior (القياس الأولى) can be taken from the chapter heading: [Condemnation of the One Who Worships Allah at a Righteous Man's Grave. What if he Worships the Man?!]

4. The two examples of the evilest of people mentioned in the ḥadīth of Ibn Mas'ūd (رَضِيَ ٱللَّهُ عَنْهُ) are; Those upon whom the last Hour comes while they are still alive and those who take graves as places of worship.

5. Masjid means the place where the prostration (worship) occurs and it also means the limbs in the body that are used to prostrate. At-Tawḥīd has to be implemented in both.

Chapter 20

1. The meaning of 'exaggeration' (الغلو) is "that which transgresses the legislated boundaries."

2. They derived Al-Lāt from 'Allāh' and al-'Uzza from Al-'Azīz.

3. By deriving the names of their idols from the beautiful names of Allāh, they dishonored His names.

4. The Messenger (صَلَّى ٱللَّهُ عَلَيْهِ وَسَلَّمَ) made dua to Allāh to protect his grave from being taken as a place of worship.

5. The wisdom behind the prohibition of exaggerating in praise of individuals is that it could lead to the evil of shirk.

Chapter 21

1. Celebration of the Prophet's birthday (صَلَّى ٱللَّهُ عَلَيْهِ وَسَلَّمَ), Christmas, New year's or anyone's birthday are examples of prohibited celebrations.

2. The narration that further emphasizes the virtues of praying non-obligatory prayers at home is the statement of the Messenger (صَلَّى ٱللَّهُ عَلَيْهِ وَسَلَّمَ): "Do not make your home graves."

3. From the characteristics of the Prophet mentioned in this chapter are; a Messenger, compassionate, merciful to the believers.

4. This and the previous chapter emphasize the protectiveness of the Messenger of at-Tawḥīd.

5. In this chapter the statement of the Messenger (صَلَّى ٱللَّٰهُ عَلَيْهِ وَسَلَّمَ): ["Do not make my grave a place of celebration ('Īd)."], is proof of the prohibition of frequenting the Prophet's grave. This is because the meaning of ('Īd) is a celebration that is frequent and recurring.

Chapter 22

1. The ṭāghūt is all that is worshipped with Allāh and is pleased to be so.

2. In this chapter, the proof for the impermissibility of following the footsteps of the Jews and Christians is the statement of Messenger (صَلَّى ٱللَّٰهُ عَلَيْهِ وَسَلَّمَ): " You will surely follow the ways of those who came before you, in everything as one arrow would to another, so much so that even if they entered a sand lizard's hole, you would enter it too."

3. Proof that Muḥammad (صَلَّى ٱللَّٰهُ عَلَيْهِ وَسَلَّمَ) is the seal of the prophets is his (صَلَّى ٱللَّٰهُ عَلَيْهِ وَسَلَّمَ) statement: "I am the finality of the Prophets. There will be no Prophet after me."

4. The saved group are the ones upon the truth; the Qur'ān and Sunnah with the understanding of the pious predecessors. With this, they are victorious and will not be harmed by the opposers or those who fail them.

5. In this chapter is a warning against the avenues that lead to shirk and that some of this Ummah will fall into worshiping idols. Therefore, studying at-Tawḥīd and implementing it is imperative. This is the relevance of this chapter to Kitāb at-Tawḥīd.

Chapter 23

1. Siḥr (magic) is sorcery performed through means which either affects the body of the afflicted, kills them, causes them illness, distorts their mind, separates a man and his wife, or causes a barrier between them.

2. The seven destroyers mentioned in the ḥadīth of Abī Hurayrah (رَضِيَ ٱللَّٰهُ عَنْهُ) are; (1) To associate partners with Allāh, (2) sorcery, (3) killing a life Allāh has forbidden to kill, (4) taking usury, (5) stealing or wasting the wealth of orphans, (6) turning your

back at the battlefield, and (7) making an accusation against chaste, unmindful women.

3. Scholars like al-Imām Aḥmad hold that the likes of the magicians intended in this chapter are disbeliever. For them to execute their sorcery, they have to display servitude (commit shirk) to the devils that aid them.

4. The mentioning of magic in this book is relevant in that magicians show servitude to the devils so their sorcery to be effective.

5. The ruler or anyone he has delegated is legislated to execute the punishment for magic.

Chapter 24

1. The connection with this chapter and the last is that the previous chapter focused on magic and its ruling. This chapter focuses on clarifying other acts which are also subcategories of magic.

2. Both the magician and the soothsayer submit and seek aid from the Shayāṭīn.

3. Like the previous chapter, this chapter is mention in this book because it opposes various affairs of at-Tawḥīd.

4. Al-'Aḍh is tale carrying.

5. Tale carrying is called magic because they both share the same result. Tale carrying, like magic, cause argumentation animosity, and division between loved ones.

Chapter 25

1. Some scholars like ibn Taymiyyah have defined an ar-Arrāf as a comprehensive term for anyone who gives information of the unseen whether it is through the devils or prediction.

2. The punishment for the one who visits a soothsayer will have his prayer rejected for forty days and nights whilst still being obliged to perform them.

3. The origins of omens is the act of basing optimism and pessimism through the movement of birds.

4. The one who visits a soothsayer and believes him has disbelieved in that which Muḥammad came with.

5. Abā Jād are letters of a sentence people wrote and they would look to the stars and claim this and that will happen (talisman – طلسم).

Chapter 26

1. An-Nushrah is the act of curing the one afflicted by magic.
2. The relevance of this chapter is that the impermissible an-Nushrah is the curing of magic through magic.
3. 'Abdullāh b. Mas'ūd (رَضِيَ اللَّهُ عَنْهُ) disliked an-Nushrah. He held it as impermissible.
4. Ibn al-Qayyim held that an-Nushrah is of two types; healing magic using magic. This is from acts of Shayṭān. The second is curing the afflicted with legislated supplications and recitations of verses from the Qur'ān.
5. The legislated method to cure the one afflicted with magic is to recite verses of the Qur'ān and medications. For every disease, there is a cure except for death.

Chapter 27

1. This chapter and the last chapter explore other acts of shirk. This chapter specifically focuses on the belief in omens.
2. An example of belief in omens mentioned in this chapter is the omen of the night owl and the omen of the month Ṣafar.
3. The belief in omens opposes trusting in Allāh.
4. Al-Fa'l is the expectation that something will occur by the permission of Allāh.
5. The belief in omens existed in the time of Mūsā (صَلَّى اللَّهُ عَلَيْهِ وَسَلَّمَ). It has been a belief of the polytheists of old.

Chapter 28

1. At-Tanjīm is the belief that stars affect occurrences.
2. At-Tanjīm is a category from the categories of magic.
3. In this chapter, the three that are threatened with not entering Jannah are; (1) the habitual alcohol drinker, (2) the believer in sorcery, and (3) the one who severs blood relations.

4. The wisdom behind the creation of the stars are three. (1) As ornaments of the heavens, (2) as missiles against the devils, and (3) As signposts for travelers.

5. The statement of the Messenger (صَلَّى ٱللَّهُ عَلَيْهِ وَسَلَّمَ): [Such a person lost his portion (on the Day of Resurrection), and has taken upon himself that which is outside his knowledge.] is proof of the impermissibility of speaking without knowledge.

Chapter 29

1. The four traits of the days of ignorance mentioned in this chapter are (1) haughtiness and boastfulness regarding one's lineage, (2) Defaming someone's lineage, (3) seeking rain through the stars, and (4) Lamentation and wailing of women for the dead.

2. Allāh swearing by is creation is proof of the lofty status of that creation.

3. Swearing by the creation is only for the creator of these creations; Allāh.

4. The statement of the Messenger (صَلَّى ٱللَّهُ عَلَيْهِ وَسَلَّمَ): "[He said, "Allāh has said, 'In this morning, some of My slaves remained true believers and some became disbelievers...] — this is proof of the affirmation of Allāh's Speech.

5. The legislated way of seeking rain is to ask Allāh (تَبَارَكَ وَتَعَالَىٰ).

END OF VOLUME ONE (Chapters 1–29)

Printed in Dunstable, United Kingdom

63800479R10176